# THE
# POLITICS
## OF THE
# EUROPEAN
# COURT
## OF
# JUSTICE

*Richard Kuper*

**KOGAN
PAGE**

Kogan Page Limited
120 Pentonville Road
London N1 9JN

© London European Research Centre,
   The University of North London 1998

Concise yet comprehensive, the Dossiers present accessible analysis of EU policies, institutions and related themes. Written by experts in the field and commissioned by the London European Research Centre of the University of North London, the European Dossiers are an invaluable source of information and interpretations for anyone with an interest in the EU.

Published five times per year, the Dossiers are available through an annual subscription or as individual titles.

Comments on the series or proposals for new titles are welcome in writing to the series editor:

Professor Michael Newman
London European Research Centre
University of North London
166–220, Holloway Road
London N7 8DB

**British Library Cataloguing in Publication Data**

ISBN  0 7494 2607 1

Typeset by JS Typesetting, Wellingborough, Northants.
Printed and bound in Great Britain by
Biddles Ltd, Guildford and King's Lynn

# Contents

# Acknowledgements

Although I had worked in the area of European Studies
for a number of years, I regarded European Community
law as an arcane and specialist area, with little wider
relevance. That was until I heard Joseph Weiler deliver
the inaugural *Journal of Common Market Studies* lecture in
Birmingham at the UACES Research Conference in
September 1995 (see Weiler, 1997, pp 97–131). I found
his talk both challenging and inspirational and was very
pleased when Michael Newman invited me to pursue my
new-found interest by giving a paper on the European
Court of Justice to the London European Research Centre
of the University of North London; I also presented it to
colleagues at the University of Hertfordshire. My thanks
to those who participated in these two seminars and, in
particular, to Michael Newman for suggesting I write it
up and extend it for this European Dossier. Thanks also
to him as well as to Irene Bruegel and Joanne Scott for
their careful reading and helpful comments on the
manuscript.

Richard Kuper
London
March 1998

# Biographical Notes

Richard Kuper was, until recently, a Senior Lecturer in Politics at the University of Hertfordshire, with special interests in democratic theory, European politics and the politics of European integration. This is reflected, not only in the production of this Dossier, but also in articles on the democratic deficit in the European Union, the making of a constitution for Europe and on concepts and practices of deliberative democracy. He has recently taken early retirement to further an interest in practical utopias, via a cooperative project for an organic farming, research and education centre in the Drôme in France. His research on the European Union continues, now focusing on the politics of biodiversity.

Dr Sonia Mazey, Churchill College, Cambridge
Dr Lee Miles, University of Hull
Dr Glenda Rosenthal, Columbia University
Dr Joanne Scott, Queen Mary and Westfield College
Professor Michael Smith, Loughborough University

# Introduction

This work offers an analysis of the European Court of Justice's activism and the role it has played in the process of European integration. A brief summary in Chapter 1 of the powers of the Court (referred to throughout with a capital 'C') is followed by a discussion in Chapter 2, of the Court's development of two key doctrines, direct effect and supremacy of European Community law, and its justification in terms of preserving the Community from ruin. Chapter 3 charts the rather stormy reception of these doctrines by the supreme courts in some member states. Chapter 4 examines the way in which lower courts and the wider legal community responded as new possibilites opened before them. In the process, some explanation is offered for what, by any account, was a series of unexpected developments. Chapter 5 turns to the Court's interventionist role in certain areas of economic integration, while Chapter 6 looks at the nature of choices the Court has made in defining key economic terms in rather narrow market-oriented ways. In conclusion, I look at some explanations for the significant political role the Court has played and consider the way in which the circumstances which have given the Court the autonomy it has are also ones which have contributed to the wider issue of the democratic deficits which so mark the European Union today.

# 1

# The Powers of the Court

The European Court of Justice is the final arbiter of disputes arising from the Community Treaties. It was originally set up under the European Coal and Steel Community Treaty, in 1951. Its formal powers are laid out in Articles 164–188 of the Treaty of Rome (as subsequently amended). It has the responsibility, as Article 164 puts it, 'to ensure that in the interpretation and application of this Treaty the law is observed'.

Today the European Court of Justice consists of 15 judges, one from each member state, assisted by 9 advocates-general, also full members of the Court, who, 'acting with complete impartiality and independence' make 'reasoned submissions' on the cases before the Court 'in order to assist' the judges. Members are appointed for six-year terms, with half the Court being replaced every three years, to ensure continuity. Reappointment is possible. The President is elected by the Court from amongst its members, for three years, and may be reappointed.

All members of the Court are, in the words of Article 167, 'persons whose independence is beyond doubt and who possess the qualifications required for appointment to the highest judicial offices in their respective countries, or who are jurisconsults of recognised competence'.

The Court normally sits as a panel of three or five judges, occasionally sitting in plenary session with a quorum of seven. Decisions are by simple majority and no dissent is recorded.

## FOUR MAIN AREAS OF JURISDICTION

1. Under Articles 169–171 failures of a member state to fulfil a Treaty obligation may be brought before the Court, by the Commission or another member state. If the state is found to be in breach of its obligations, it is required 'to take the necessary measures to comply with the judgment'. Since the Treaty on European Union (the Maastricht Treaty) came into effect in November 1993, the Court has real teeth, with the power to impose penalty payments on member states.

2. The Court has extensive powers of judicial review of Community acts (Articles 173, 174, 176). It is empowered to review the 'legality' of regulations, directives and decisions adopted by the Council and the Commission, and some acts of the European Central Bank and the European Parliament. Grounds for review include lack of competence, procedural infringements, or general misuse of powers. The Court may declare an offending act void and require the offending institution to take the 'necessary measures to comply with' its judgment.

3. Under Articles 175–176, the Court can deal with a failure to act on the part of the Commission, Council or European Parliament, such action being brought by one of the institutions of the Community. Once again, the offending institution may be required to take the 'necessary measures'.

4. Under Article 177 the Court was given jurisdiction to give 'preliminary rulings' about the interpretation of the Treaty, or the validity or interpretation of an act of any Community institution. Where such a question is raised before a national court, that court may (and, if it is a final court with no appeal beyond, *must*) ask the ECJ for a preliminary ruling. A substantial part of the history of the Court is concerned with the development of its jurisdiction under this procedure.

# 2

# The Process of Constitutionalisation

One of the most significant claims made for the Court of Justice is that it has single-handedly transformed what was a traditional international agreement into the constitution of a quasi-federal Europe. There is no doubting the significance of such a claim and as I shall show below, there is a good deal of truth in the qualitative changes that the Court has wrought in the nature of the Community. It is unwise, however, to take such claims at face value. In this section I shall follow through the conventional presentation of the development of Community legal doctrine in this area. I shall, however, also qualify it, identifying the strong opposition which continues to be expressed to it at very senior levels of the judiciary, in France, Germany and elsewhere. In conclusion, I shall also question the meaning of constitutionalisation which is assumed in this analysis.

Academic analysis of this development starts with Eric Stein's classic analysis (1981, p 1) which begins:

> *Tucked away in the fairyland Duchy of Luxembourg and blessed, until recently, with benign neglect by the powers that be and the mass media, the Court of Justice of the European Communities has fashioned a constitutional framework for a federal-type structure in Europe.*

A forceful endorsement of this view is found in an article in 1989 by G Federico Mancini (1991, p 178), a member of the European Court of Justice, where he claimed that the Court 'has sought to "constitutionalise" the Treaty [of Rome], to fashion a constitutional framework for a quasi-federal structure in Europe'. This has been achieved by the establishment by the Court of a series of doctrines, most notably those of direct effect and supremacy of EC over national law.

What is really at stake in the development of these doctrines is the question of enforceability of the obligations established by the Treaty. It is generally the case that enforcement mechanisms in traditional treaties are weak – one has only to think of the effect of United Nations resolutions on Iraq or Israel, for example. The Treaty of Rome did establish certain means of redress. The Commission can initiate action under Article 169, while a member state can do so under Article 170. Even if successful, however, the remedies granted under Article 171 of the Treaty of Rome were very limited. A situation where the Commission is constantly suing the governments of the member states, or they are suing each other, is unlikely to be one which encourages constructive cooperation in other areas.

The introduction and development of the doctrine of direct effect was to dramatically transform the way in which Community norms have come to be enforced, by allowing them to be appealed to directly in actions before national courts. As Weiler (1982, pp 45–6) puts it:

> *Under traditional international law governments which breach their obligations are only subject to intergovernmental remedies or, at most, intergovernmental suit before international tribunals. As a result of direct effect, breach by a government of Community law becomes a breach of its own law with remedies lying before its national courts.*

How was this transformation brought about? The doctrine of direct effect was first enunciated in the *Van Gend en Loos* case in 1963, which established that certain Treaty articles could be relied on by individuals in national courts. The actual case in point hinged around Article 12 which forbids member states from 'introducing between themselves any new customs duties on imports or exports or charges having similar effect'. Advocate-General Roemer argued that this Article was too complex to be enforced directly and that allowing national courts to interpret it would not lead to any uniformity of application. The Court decided otherwise.

The Court, in its ruling, was quite explicit:

> *the Community constitutes a new legal order of international law for the benefit of which the states have limited their sovereign rights, albeit within limited fields, and the subjects of which comprise not only member states but also their nationals. Community law therefore not only imposes obligations on individuals but is also intended to confer upon them rights which become part of their legal heritage. These rights arise not only where they are expressly granted by the Treaty, but also by reason of obligations which the Treaty imposes in a clearly defined way upon individuals as well as upon member states and upon the institutions of the Community.*

The story of the direct effect doctrine is one of how its remit was slowly extended. Before taking that up, however, it is necessary to look at the related doctrine of the supremacy of EC law which emerged in the case of *Costa* v *ENEL* the following year. This is indeed already hinted at in *Van Gend* (1963); but in *Costa* the Court was faced with a reference from an Italian court which concerned an alleged conflict between some Treaty provisions and a subsequent Italian statute, nationalising an electricity company of which Costa was a shareholder. The Court's decision was uncompromising:

> *The reception, within the laws of each member state, of provisions having a Community source, and more particularly of the terms and of the spirit of the Treaty, has as a corollary the impossibility, for the member state, to give reference to a unilateral and subsequent measure against a legal order accepted by them on the basis of reciprocity . . . The transfer, by member states, from their national orders in favour of the Community order of the rights and obligations arising from the Treaty, carries with it a clear limitation of their sovereign rights upon which a subsequent unilateral law, incompatible with the aims of the Community, cannot prevail.*

These two doctrines, direct effect and supremacy of EC law, complement one another and, taken together, clearly have a powerful federalising effect, establishing a hierarchy of legal norms and a uniformity of application throughout the Community. This has been heightened by the way in which, in the years following *Van Gend* (1963), the reach of direct effect has been extended.

First, more Treaty Articles have been found to have direct effect. In *Walgrave and Koch* (1974) Article 7 (now Article 6) prohibiting any discrimination on the grounds of nationality was held to bind directly not just member states but individuals as well, as was Treaty Article 119 on equal pay, in *Defrenne No 2* (1976). Second, the Court turned to secondary legislation and Article 189 of the Treaty, which lays down the status of various kinds of Community legal instrument. Regulations are described there as being 'directly applicable', which would appear to differentiate them from other forms of secondary legislation. In *Franz Grad* (1970), however, decisions were also held to be directly effective, a relatively noncontroversial development in terms of their description in Article 189 as 'binding in their entirety' on those to whom they are addressed. But when it comes to directives there is a *prima facie* argument that they should not have direct effect, for, by contrast with regulations, directives are described merely as 'binding, as to the result to be achieved, but . . . the choice of form and methods' is left open to the national authorities. In *Van Duyn* (1974) the Court addressed the issue. Van Duyn, a Dutch national, was refused entry to the UK to take up work with the Church of Scientology and challenged the grounds for her exclusion under Article 3 of Directive 64/221. The Court upheld her right to invoke this directive in a national court. There were conditions attached to this direct effect: the legal instruments had to be sufficiently clear and precise, and unconditional, leaving no room for discretion in implementation, conditions which were held to be fulfilled once the time-limits that states had been given for the implementation of directives had expired. Furthermore, the direct effect produced was apparently restricted to 'vertical' direct effect, in other words, to the enforcement of obligations laid by directives on member states and not able of themselves to impose obligations on individuals. This Court interpretation was confirmed in *Marshall* (1986) where, while the state was given a broad definition (to include public bodies acting in their capacity as employers), so-called 'horizontal' direct effect was not accepted. Invited to reconsider in *Faccini Dori* (1994), and with Advocate-General Lenz urging that the principle of direct effect should allow for the enforcement of directives against all parties, the Court nonetheless refused.

However, as the Court pointed out, other remedies are at hand. In *Von Colson* (1984) the Court had established a principle of 'indirect effect' by ruling that member states' courts had to interpret national law so as to ensure that the objectives of directives are achieved (as part of the general obligation under Article 5 of the Treaty, which requires states to 'take all appropriate measures' to ensure fulfilment of their Treaty obligations). In *Marleasing* (1990) the Court specifically ruled that national courts were 'required' to interpret domestic law in such a way as to ensure that the objectives of directives were achieved – even where no national implementing measure had been introduced at all. But, recognising that national courts might find it difficult to interpret directives in this way when they were in conflict with the 'wording and evident intention of the legislature' (as the German Supreme Labour Court put it in 1992 in refusing to read the German Labour Code to comply with the Equal Treatment Directive), the Court held in *Kolpinguis Nijmegen* (1987) that national courts' obligations were 'limited by the general principles of law which form part of Community law, in particular the principles of legal certainty and non-retroactivity' (both cited in Steiner & Wood, 1996, p 53) or even, that an alternative remedy might have to be found.

This was soon at hand, fashioned by the Court in *Francovich* (1991) which held that, under certain specified conditions, responsibility for non-implementation of a directive should rest fully on the state, against which individuals could seek compensation. The extent of a state's obligation was not, however, limited to directives but, the judgment implied, extended to enforcement of Community law generally; how far was clarified in *Factortame* (1993) as meaning 'manifest and serious' breaches of Community law. Case law is still evolving as to what constitutes a 'serious breach'.

The result of the steady increase in the remit of direct (and indirect) effect was to enmesh national legal systems ever more in the emerging European Community legal system. What has to be explained is why and to what extent these national legal systems have been willing to be so enmeshed. Before turning to those questions directly, a little more needs to be said about the second doctrine the Court has enunciated, that of the supremacy of EC law. At one level it can be seen simply as a corollary of taking the doctrine of direct effect seriously. Clearly, if any member state could simply pass a law invalidating Treaty provisions, no new legal order would have been established. Equally clearly, however, the value of a doctrine of supremacy depends not simply on the Court declaring it, but on the courts in member states accepting and acting upon it.

Here, indeed, there was an extended and ongoing resistance on at least two levels: a specific objection focused on the implications for the constitutional protection of human rights, which were written into the German and Italian constitutions and which might be threatened by this doctrine, and a more general one focused on the nature of the doctrine itself, a resistance which continues to simmer in important places. It may, perhaps, have been the case that the general doctrine was widely viewed with disfavour and the issue of human rights became the front line of resistance to it. The way the Court dealt with the specific issue of rights is instructive.

The issue emerged in *Stauder* (1969), and again in the case of *Internationale Handelsgesellschaft* (1970) which hinged on a claim that an EC regulation infringed the principle of proportionality, enshrined in the German Federal constitution, to the effect that action must be proportionate to the aim that is to be achieved. Here the Court was uncompromising, declaring that law arising from the Treaty of Rome could not

> *have the courts opposing to it rules of national law of any nature whatsoever... The validity of a Community instrument or its effect within a member state cannot be affected by allegations that it strikes at either the fundamental rights as formulated in that State's constitution or the principles of a national constitutional structure.*

Such a bald declaration might have been seen as a declaration of war against fundamental rights as protected by member states' constitutions, but the Court gave comfort by declaring that one of the principal aims of the Community was respect for such rights. In a series of further judgments the nature and source of these rights were clarified. In *Nold* (1974), a coal wholesaler sought to challenge a decision taken under the European Coal and Steel Community (ECSC) as in breach of his company's fundamental right to free pursuit of its business activity. The Court took the opportunity of clarifying its position. It found that it was

> *bound to draw inspiration from constitutional traditions common to the member states, and it cannot therefore uphold measures which are incompatible with fundamental rights recognised and protected by the constitutions of those states. Similarly, international treaties for the protection of human rights on which the member states have collaborated or of which they are signatories, can supply guidelines which should be followed within the framework of Community law.*

The most important such treaty is obviously the European Convention for the Protection of Human Rights and Fundamental Freedoms, to which all member states are signatories. Subsequent cases have established other possible sources of similar general principles such as the European Social Charter and Convention 11 of the International Labour Organisation.

Having given reassurances about the human rights implications of the principle of supremacy, its reach was extended steadily over time. In *Simmenthal* (1979) the Court explained to an Italian judge that EC law had to be enforced immediately, even before his own Constitutional Court had had an opportunity to declare an Italian law which conflicted with EC law invalid. The reasoning is instructive:

> *any recognition that national legislative measures which encroach upon the field within which the Community exercises its legislative power or which are otherwise*

*incompatible with the provisions of Community law had any legal effect would amount to a corresponding denial of the effectiveness of obligations undertaken unconditionally and irrevocably by member states pursuant to the Treaty and would thus imperil the very foundations of the Community.*

It was, indeed, the same principle to be applied in *Factortame* (1993), mentioned earlier, in which British courts were advised to grant interim relief to Spanish fishermen while the issue as to whether English law was in breach of EC law or not was resolved, and that the rule of national law which prevented the granting of such relief should be set aside.

Linked to the concept of supremacy is that of preemption, whereby once the Community has acquired an exclusive right to make law in an area, a member state is no longer able to legislate in that area. Thus, for instance, the very existence of the Common Agricultural Policy precludes member states legislating in the area. In a challenge to an international road transport agreement to which the EEC was a party, the Court decided in *ERTA* (1971) that once the Community, in implementing a common policy, lays down common rules, member states were no longer able, individually or collectively, to undertake obligations with third countries. In the eighties, in relation to the North Sea fisheries, 'the Court held that member states were no longer at liberty to enact conservation laws, even though no Community measures had been taken' (Mancini, 1991, p 183).

Thus a series of doctrines with wider and wider implications has been slowly established by the Court of Justice over four decades. Its own view of what it has done has clarified over time and in *Les Verts* (1986) it had no difficulty in referring to the Treaty as 'the basic constitutional charter' of the Community. It elaborated this in its Opinion on the Draft Agreement on a European

Economic Area (1991) when it declared that 'the EEC Treaty, albeit concluded in the form of an international agreement, nonetheless constitutes the constitutional charter of a Community based on the rule of law' (Weatherill, 1995, 184).

In his 1981 analysis, Eric Stein showed how the Court had overwhelmingly followed the lead of the Commission in all the important cases concerned with direct effect and supremacy. The main opposition had come from national governments, entitled to make representations to the Court in Article 177 hearings.

This story is one in which the Commission, charged as it is in the Treaty (Article 155) to ensure the proper functioning and development of the common market, is required to 'ensure that the provisions of this Treaty and the measures taken by the institutions pursuant thereto are applied'. The Court, likewise, is there to ensure that 'the law is observed' in the interpretation and application of the Treaty (Article 164). The Court and the Commission are thus situated as guardians of the Community and its objectives, institutionally inclined to a broad view of Community competences. The Court is further aided by working within a teleological tradition that, as Timothy Bainbridge and Anthony Teasdale put it (Bainbridge & Teasdale, 1995, pp 99–100):

> allows the 'ultimate purpose' of a piece of legislation to be taken into consideration. This means that it is entirely legitimate, with respect to a particular text, to take not only the exact purpose of the words into account, but also anything that may usefully and convincingly be adduced about the intention behind the words.

At stake is how far such 'teleological' interpretation can go. Hjalte Rasmussen (1986), in a trailblazing and biting critique of the Court, argued that: 'It is widely known but rarely recorded in print that even firm believers in a federal Europe occasionally are baffled by the Court's strong and bold pro-Community policy preferences.' While seeing the Court as one of the chief architects in the early days, protecting the nascent Community from crumbling 'under the weight of growing parochialism', he felt that the moral authority of the Court was now threatened by too much political jurisprudence, which, in the absence of its own means of enforcement, might 'become fatal in the Community' (Rasmussen, 1986, pp 3, 8, 9).

Joseph Weiler gives an academic interpretation of the original Treaties as

> *traditional multipartite international treaties. Although including certain novel institutional features, they were, in line with precedent, expected to be interpreted in accordance with the normal canons of treaty interpretation, one of which is a presumption against loss of sovereignty by states.* (Weiler, 1982a, p 270)

*Van Gend* provides a good example of how open-ended interpretation can become if one takes possible intentions into account. The defences filed by three states, Germany, Belgium and the Netherlands, and the Advocates-General's opinion all argued that 'from all they knew about the intentions of those who drafted the Treaty . . . Articles such as Article 12 were not destined to have direct effects' (Rasmussen, 1986, p 12). However, it was not those expectations the Court relied on. Rather it saw its task as following other intentions, expressed in the need to secure the overall objectives of the Treaty and this, it reckoned, required direct effect.

The justification for this lies in Article 5 of the Treaty:

> *Member states shall take all appropriate measures, whether general or particular, to ensure fulfilment of the obligations arising out of this Treaty or resulting from*

*action taken by the institutions of the Community. They
shall facilitate the achievement of the Community's tasks.
They shall abstain from any measure which could
jeopardise the attainment of the objectives of this Treaty.*

The scope of this article 'is theoretically vast, if not
infinite . . . What Article 5 has done,' as Ian Ward (1996a,
p 65) claims, 'is effectively to enable the ECJ to construct
any rationale for any decision it likes.'

That is not to say that the Court's decisions in general
are arbitrary; quite the reverse. The Court always, and
inevitably as a court of law, desires to give an acceptable
and convincing legalistic justification for its decisions. It
is just that the framework provided by something like
Article 5 is so broad that in certain cases, decisions are so
unpredictable as to be perceived as fairly arbitrary.
Rasmussen, for instance, while unhappy with the *Van Gend*
reading of Article 12, was prepared to accept it as a
legitimate reading. However, the Court's interpretation
of Article 189(3) giving direct effect to directives was one,
he felt, which 'went way beyond the textual stipulations
of that Article . . . To many a European lawyer this is
revolting judicial behaviour' (Rasmussen, 1986, p 12).

Arbitrary, in terms of the law, but not necessarily
unpredictable politically – a view borne out by looking at
some of the early Court judges' own views as to what they
thought they were up to. Robert Lecourt's *L'Europe des
Juges* (1976), for instance, is described by Rasmussen as a
eulogy for the Court. In it, Lecourt justifies what the judges
had done, in terms of what would have followed had
they not. 'Ruin' or its synonyms are used extensively by
Lecourt who explains (Lecourt, 1976, p 222, author's
translation):

*The goal envisaged thus demanded an autonomous
juridical system, a community of legal rules distinct from
national law and safeguarded in its unity against any*

14

*centrifugal threat. [This, he continues, is] proclaimed by
no text, but the entire law of the Communities is conceived
and organised in this way.*

Similarly Pierre Pescatore, judge and law professor, is if
anything even more explicit in *The Law of Integration*
(1974). The search for economic and political union, while
a distant aim, should be seen

> *as the completion of a conception left incomplete in the
> Treaty of Rome. Even if this project still seems far from
> achievement, it has the advantage of enabling us hence-
> forth to envisage the evolution of the Community in the
> light of a coherent and complete plan.* (Pescatore, 1974,
> pp 22–3)

In moving in this direction,

> *the judicial element reveals in the Community context
> extraordinary dynamism and fertility. Without exagger-
> ation, one might speak of a genuine revelation of the
> possibilities of the judicial element, once it is permitted
> to play fully and freely its proper role in the context of a
> system of integration.* (Pescatore, 1974, p 83)

The way this is achieved is through what he calls its
'constructive methods of interpretation', which have two
elements, the systematic and the teleological. The former
is merely the deduction of specific rules from the general
scheme of the Treaties and subsequent legislation. What
Pescatore has to say of teleological interpretation is
perhaps more interesting:

> *Contrary to a widespread idea, this is not simply 'one
> method among others'. The rule of law being by its nature
> a provision with a certain objective, the teleological*

*method is, in the last analysis, the decisive criterion of every legal interpretation. This is doubly true in the context of treaties which proceed by laying down objectives rather than substantive rules.* (Pescatore, 1974, p 88)

Pescatore, writing well over a decade before *Francovich*, envisaged sanctions and reparations as a likely development of the case law of direct effect with member states liable for their faults to each other and the Community as a whole (Pescatore, 1974, pp 104–5).

So too Kutscher, in a speech on taking over as president-elect of the Court in 1976, declared:

> *The principle of the progressive integration of the member states in order to attain the objectives of the Treaty does not only comprise a political requirement; it amounts rather to a Community legal principle which the Court of Justice has to bear in mind when interpreting Community law, if it is to discharge in a proper manner its allotted task of upholding the law when it interprets and applies the Treaties.*

In other words its interpretation has to be 'dynamic and teleological' (Kutscher, in Rasmussen, 1986, p 180).

Both Kutscher and Pescatore gave added political justification for the Court's dynamic approach in the face of the legislative inertia of both Council and Commission. Pescatore, for instance, recognising the action of the Court as 'bold', sees it as partly coinciding with 'certain periods of crisis and stagnation in the sphere of action of the political institutions' (Pescatore, in Rasmussen, 1986, p 178).

Rasmussen's argument is convincing, both in his view of the Preamble and Article 2 as guidelines destined for political consumption, not statements of intent having a fundamental priority over all others and in his view that, if judges are acting teleologically they should take them together with

> *all expressions of will which the Founding Fathers laid down in the Treaty, including those less powerful integration promoting ones to be found in fairly many of the operational Articles of the Treaties.* (Rasmussen, 1986, p 183)

Rasmussen was criticised at the time by those who argued that founding intent is always intangible. This is true, but Rasmussen has been more than vindicated by the work of Alan Milward and his colleagues (1993) in the archives of member states. This has established beyond reasonable doubt that integration and the surrender of a degree of national sovereignty which the Treaty of Rome represented, was not

> *the intellectual counter-current to European nationalism, which it is so often said to represent, but [. . .] a further stage in the reassertion of the role of the nation state. The common policies of the European Community came into being in the attempt to uphold and stabilise the post-war consensus on which the European nation state was rebuilt. They were a part of the rescue of the nation state.* (Milward, 1993, p 44)

If the view that the founding fathers' prime intention was for long-term political union is overblown, so too is the argument used frequently of 'the impending ruin of the Community' but for the Court's intervention (Mancini, 1994, p 181). Stephen Weatherill (1995) provides a nice summary when he writes that:

> *The Court has regularly confirmed its view that the EC system can retain its integrity only provided that Community law holds supremacy over conflicting*

*national law. Without that basic hierarchy, disintegration would follow. Even one breach in the dam would be too many, for one fissure would inevitably breed others.* (Weatherill, 1995, p 104)

This slippery-slope style argument is notoriously tricky. Apart from assuming an inevitability of decline, it also assumes that historical processes are simple to divine and easy to intervene in. There is no conception of unintended consequences – or even of political compromise – which together provide a far more effective starting point for historical analysis of Community development. Indeed, the anger which underpins Rasmussen's (1986) analysis of the Court derives from his fear of more and more judges and other lawyers of members states coming to see the Court as 'intolerably activist', as a result of which the Court was losing authority – and the Community momentum.

Perhaps what the above establishes most of all is the intangibility of generalised intentions and the need to move from a moralistic evaluation of the Court's activities – whether or not it has exceeded its powers – to a more directly political and institutional one. It is not that the former is unimportant; indeed when considering what kind of Community is being built, putative citizens of that Community need to take its ethical dimensions very seriously. Equally, history cannot be written as the story of bold visions and betrayals – though both of these have their place in any analysis. The real problem is to make sense of why bold visions won out (if they did), how the betrayers got away with it (if they did). An altogether more interesting and complex story emerges.

# 3

# Reception of the Court's Doctrines by Supreme Courts

The ways in which national courts responded to the growing assertion of powers by the ECJ were varied. The Benelux courts seem to have been untroubled by these developments unlike the courts in France, Germany and Italy in the 1960s. In these latter countries, there has been an institutional and doctrinal struggle over decades, not fully resolved to this day. There may now be broad acceptance of the Court's authority and rulings in the fields of competences recognised, but there is neither consensus about the extent of these competences nor about who is the final adjudicator.

Mancini presents a complacent view that 'the Court's supremacy doctrine was accepted by the judiciaries and the administrations of both the original and the new member states, with the exception of some grumblings by the French Conseil d'État, the Italian Corte Costituzionale, and a couple of English law lords' (Mancini, 1961, p 180). He acknowledges 'bitter opposition in many quarters' to the extension of direct effect to directives, though he doubts that this warrants 'the revolt staged by the Conseil d'État or the Bundesfinanzhof' (1991, p 183). Talk of 'revolts' of course alerts us to the fact that acceptance has not been as straightforward as Mancini suggests. Nor should this be surprising. As Karen Alter (1996) points out, there is a general doctrine to the effect that the latest law trumps all previous law – including international treaties. To the extent that the Treaty of Rome was an international treaty, there could be no question of supremacy. Indeed, as Alter remarks, 'to this day no national judiciary has accepted the reasoning offered by the ECJ (in *Costa*, (1964)) as legal basis for EC law supremacy' (Alter, 1996, p 462). For the French and the British, for example, EC supremacy violates notions of parliamentary sovereignty and/or the general will; for the Germans or the Irish, it threatens provisions of their national constitutions. How has this conflict been played out in practice?

The case of France is an interesting one in that two of its three supreme courts, the Conseil d'État and the Conseil Constitutionnel have openly defied the ECJ (see Rasmussen, 1986; Phelan, 1997; Plötner cited in Mattli & Slaughter, 1996). Because of its peculiar place in the constitution and the need to comment on the legality of any proposed law before it is finally passed through parliament, the Conseil Constitutionnel is not to be found making (or refusing to make) Article 177 references. Nonetheless its December 1976 affirmation that the French constitution did not warrant a transfer of sovereignty, in whole or in part, to any international organisation is in direct opposition to *Costa* (Rasmussen, 1986, p 308).

But day by day it is the Conseil d'État, the supreme court of the administrative law jurisdiction, and the Cour de Cassation, the supreme court of the civil and criminal jurisdictions, which are largely responsible for the policing of the implications of international treaties (Phelan, 1997, p 255).

The Cour de Cassation is generally held to have accepted EC law, resistance coming solely from the Conseil d'État. Alas, it is not so simple. In French law there is a presumption of a separation of powers, to the extent that it is an offence for a court to challenge the validity of a law duly passed by the Assembly. Treaties are generally regarded as of equal status to laws and therefore the Cour de Cassation would normally give precedence to laws which post-dated a treaty. This position was reversed in the case of *Société des cafés Jacques Vabre* (1975) which is generally held to have established the superiority of EC law by holding that Article 95 (EEC) had an authority superior even to posterior laws. In its judgment, the Court affirmed:

> *considering that the Treaty of 25 March 1957, which, in virtue of [Article 55] of the constitution, has an authority superior to* lois *[statutes], institutes its own juridical order integrated into those of the member states; that in reason of this specificity, the juridical order which it has created is directly applicable to nationals of these States and binds their jurisdictions.* (Cited in Phelan, 1997, p 266)

Phelan describes this reasoning, quite understandably, as 'enigmatic'. In reaching its judgment the Court did not accept the opinion of its Procureur générale Touffait who had urged acceptance of the *Costa* reasoning. Instead its decision was 'a fudge', based on both French constitutional and EC law grounds.

> *The reference to Article 55 applies only to superiority. The legal basis for direct effect differs from the legal basis for supremacy, a conclusion which is at variance both with EC law and French constitutional law as expounded by the Conseil Constitutionnel.* (Phelan, 1997, p 264)

It also differs from the Conseil d'État's reasoning in *Nicolo* (1989) which we will shortly return to.

So, in purely legal terms there is an extremely odd situation, one in which Phelan argues that the Cour de Cassation's friendlier reasoning may conceivably be reversed, there being a constitutional obligation (Article

21

62) on it to be faithful to French constitutional law's interpretation of the limits of EC law and a legal system in which pressure from lower courts may encourage a change of mind (Phelan, 1997, pp 268-9).

Be that as it may, with the case of the Conseil d'État there has been outright rebellion, with a refusal to ask for any preliminary rulings, apparently on the grounds that it 'has its own ideas about what Community law ought to be'. In many cases it has 'acted in open violation of a basic EC law principle as laid down by the Court of Justice . . . The Conseil d'État, by implication, criticises the EC Court for usurping legislative or even constitution-making power' (Rasmussen, 1986, p 310).

The classic case, dating from 1978, is *Cohn-Bendit*. Here the Paris Administrative Court decided to seek a ruling from the ECJ as to whether the French Ministry of the Interior was in contravention of Community law (Article 48 and Directive 64/221) in refusing entry to Daniel Cohn-Bendit to take up employment in France. The Conseil argued, in precise opposition to the direct effects of the relevant parts of the directive as determined by the ECJ, that Directive 64/221 was irrelevant to the case and quashed the reference. (The French government lifted its ban so the disputed issues did not have to be fought to a conclusion . . .) (Phelan, 1997, pp 311–12).

The Conseil's prolonged refusal to apply EC law over a conflicting national law was finally reversed in the *Nicolo* case (1989). This case concerned the compatibility of French legislative provisions with Article 227(1) EEC, ie with a Treaty provision. In rapid order cases were decided which extended this to other legal instruments: *Boisdet* (1990) to the primacy to regulations; and in *Rothmans* and *Philip Morris* (the *Cigarette Cases* (1992)) to directives. But the decision was not grounded in any simple accept-ance of the supremacy of EC law. Rather, Article 55 of the French constitution, which gives EC law a superior authority, had been effectively ranked above the constit-utional principle of the separation of powers, as it had formerly interpreted. As Phelan points out, this reasoning is internal to French constitutional law. It is worth quoting him at some length on this question as he sets out the reasoning advanced in the opinion of Government Commissioner Freydman, which was followed in *Nicolo* (1989):

> *European Community law is public international law and is to be treated thus; its status in French law is a result of Article 55; conflict between the European Community treaty and another treaty is to be resolved by the application of the Vienna Convention; observance of all public international law is conditional upon satisfaction of the condition of reciprocity which may necessitate the seeking of the opinion of the Minister for Foreign Affairs; to base the control by the Conseil d'État of the compatibility of* lois *with European Community law on the specificity of the latter would be 'the worst of solutions . . . without* any *legal basis'. The Government Commissioner referred expressly to the* Costa v. ENEL *and* Simmenthal *line of Court of Justice jurisprudence in order to state:*
>
> *'We do not believe that you can follow the Court in this Praetorian jurisprudence which, in truth, appears to us at least criticisable. To do this you would engage in effect in a logic, difficult to justify, of* supranationality *. . . which would lead . . . to the holding of this treaty [of Rome] definitively unconstitutional.'* (Phelan, 1997, pp 262–3)

Similarly, with regard to directives, Government Commissioner Laroque in the *Cigarette Cases* accepted them as binding (because they are public international law) 'without going so far as to confirm the conception of absolute primacy of Community law . . . as the Court of Justice . . . understands it' (cited in Phelan, 1997, p263). And the Court reaffirmed in its *Compagnie Générale des*

*Eaux* decision, 23 July 1993, that individuals still do not have rights established under directives that are directly effective against the state (Phelan, 1997, p 264).

I have gone into the French case at length because it is an example of profound disagreement as to the nature and extent to which European law can and should be applied within national jurisdictions. The situation in Britain offers many parallels. Although there has been an increased willingness over time to accept the effective superiority of EU Law, constitutional lawyers still generally seem to 'adhere to the orthodox position that the binding effect of EC law in the UK flows only from the European Communities Act 1972, an Act which Parliament remains as free to repeal as any other Act, although for the time being it chooses not to' (Shaw, 1996, p 260). The situation in Ireland is similar, the obligation to be bound by EC law deriving from the 1972 Act which is similarly repealable. In any event, 'Irish constitutional law has a different perspective as to what constitutes European Community law from European Community law's self-description' (Phelan, 1997, p 352).

What the French case also shows, however, as do a series of House of Lords judgments in the 1990s (Shaw, 1996, pp 296–9), is the increased willingness of national supreme courts to try to find ways of responding to the steady pressure to accept a widened remit for European law. One has the rather odd situation of a *de facto* triumph of EC law in most day-to-day circumstances with a substantial theoretical gulf in the reasons advanced for its acceptance.

Does it matter? The answer, perhaps unfortunately, is yes, that it matters profoundly. It does so for a number of reasons. One is internal to law and legal doctrine itself, or at least to that version which is propagated by the Court of Justice, which is founded upon a notion of internal coherence (though postmodern critiques are calling the reality – and possibility – of this into question (Ward, 1996a)). The notion that EU law is being implemented merely because it has been (provisionally) adopted as part of national law is difficult to reconcile with a justification for obedience to it which derives from 'its inherent qualities as interpreted by the Court of Justice using the theory of the transfer of sovereign rights' (Shaw, 1996, p 296). It always remains possible for national courts to revise their own views as to the extent of competences delegated to the EU and therefore as to how far EU law is legitimately part of national law. Lest this seem academic, this is precisely what was hinted at by no less a court than the German Constitutional Court in the *Brunner* case in 1993, discussed below.

A second reason for concern is that there are fundamental political issues at stake, ones which cannot – and will not – be solved by some legalistic sleight of hand. The EU has suffered greatly by being built behind the backs of its citizenry, as it were. The problem is now widely recognised and encapsulated in the expression 'democratic deficit', though there are widely divergent diagnoses as to its extent and ways of dealing with it (see Kuper, 1998; Newman, 1996; Gustavsson, 1998). It is also widely accepted that a non-elected body which deliberates in secret – the Court of Justice – has played a highly interventionist and activist role in the development of the Community to date. 'In fact,' affirms Ward, 'the ECJ has uniformly and consistently been the most effective integrative institution in the Community' (1996a, p 52). What is increasingly called into question is the legitimacy of what has happened, a question posed sharply by Weiler and colleagues recently, when they asked: 'By what authority, if any – in the vocabulary of normative political theory – can the claim of European law to be both constitutionally superior and with immediate effect in the polity be sustained?' (Weiler, Haltern and Mayer, 1995, p 10). The answer, at best, is 'not easily'.

In the context of challenges to the Court's authority, a recent case goes to the heart of this question of legitimacy. The German Constitutional Court was faced with a challenge by Manfred Brunner, Munich lawyer and former *chef de cabinet* of the EC Commission, as to whether signing the Maastricht Treaty (and establishing a monetary union) was compatible with the national democratic account-ability demanded by the German Federal Constitution. It is a task which Sverker Gustavsson has described as squaring the circle (Gustavsson, 1998). As he shows, the Federal Court tried to do just that, finding such a compatibility by means of a complex argument: that the suprastatism established in the first pillar was provisional, with sovereignties delegated, not surrendered, and with the competences delegated both marginal in relation to the functioning of German democracy as a whole and predictable in their use at the European level. What is of particular interest here is not the precise details of the argument (though it is hard to see the situation arising out of full-scale EMU as provisional, marginal or pre-dictable) but the Federal Court's representation of the Community and its legal order as, in Jo Shaw's terms, 'fundamentally a creature of international relations and international law, based on Treaties which are controlled by the member states, and lacking the *sui generis* features of supranationalism which the Court of Justice has always claimed for it' (Shaw, 1996, p 65) – indeed since *Van Gend* (1963)! Implicit in the judgment, too, is the devastating assumption that the limits to Community legislative powers are as much a matter of German constitutional law and by implication, therefore, of the constitutional law of all other member states as of Community law (Weiler et al, 1995, p 36). The Community was defined by the German court as an association of sovereign states (a *Staatenverbund*) with limited competences and, most significantly, lacking competence-competence, ie the power to determine the scope of its competences. This power, it implied, lay with the Federal Court and other national constitutional courts. With one fell swoop the settlement over the question of fundamental rights protected by the German constitution, seemingly resolved by the Federal Court bowing to the ECJ, has been once more called into question. (Shaw, 1996, pp 64–6). Indeed, the Brunner case seems to have encouraged litigation before the Federal Court. A particularly interesting case is to be brought before the Court in 1998, challenging Germany's right to proceed with EMU since it is claimed not to have met the conditions laid down in the Treaty On European Union. The issue of supremacy has by no means yet been resolved.

# 4

# Reception by Lower Courts and the Wider Legal Community

In the previous section, high-level opposition to what can be described, at least in part, as 'a narrative of plain and simple judicial empowerment' (Weiler, 1991, p 2426) has been discussed and the argument made that at this fundamental level the deepest issues remain to be resolved. At the same time it was made clear that there is an extraordinarily widespread day-to-day acceptance both of the Courts' jurisprudence and of EU law as part of national law. No one would have anticipated such an outcome in 1957.

The description given previously of Article 5 may suggest that the Court can do anything. In reality there are enormous institutional constraints on the Court's powers. In particular, the Court can only respond to cases which come before it; its rulings can, as we have seen, be ignored by national courts; and, finally, it is not immune to having its wings clipped and its powers curbed by the process of intergovernmental reform. From this point of view, the question must be how the Court has managed to succeed at all.

Here the Court has to be seen as a deft political actor. Hartley's description of its mode of operating in cases that might represent a challenge to the interests of national governments has not been bettered:

> *A common tactic is to introduce a new doctrine gradually:
> in the first case that comes before it, the Court will establish
> the doctrine as a general principle but suggest that it is
> subject to various qualifications; the Court may even find
> some reason why it should not be applied to the particular
> facts of the case. The principle, however, is now estab-
> lished. If there are not too many protests, it will be re-
> affirmed in later cases; the qualifications can then be
> whittled away and the full extent of the doctrine revealed.*
> (Hartley, 1994, pp 87–8)

Burley & Mattli (1993) describe this process as one of
shifting expectations:

> *As long as those actors to which the Court's decisions are
> directed – member state governments, national courts,
> and individuals – accept one decision as a statement of
> existing law and proceed to make their arguments in the
> next case from that benchmark, they are shifting their
> expectations.* (Burley & Mattli, 1993, p 67)

The Court, moving slowly, has generally been very
successful in achieving this shift.

The process can be seen in the limited nature of the
direct effect mooted in *Van Gend* (1963). Before any Treaty
article could be regarded as directly effective it had in
the words of the Court to be 'unconditional, legally perfect
and henceforward capable of being applied by the national
courts', tight enough conditions to reduce, if not remove,
fears. 'In political terms direct effect would still be
presented as exceptional, and hence member state disquiet
at the development could be minimised' (Craig, 1992,
p 460). The story of the direct effect doctrine is one of
how limitations upon it were slowly stripped away. Not
until ten years after *Van Gend* was it suggested that
directives, too, could have direct effect.

There is a fiction in International Relations theory that states can be treated as unified entities: Germany wants, Britain stands for... Similarly, even within states, particular institutions are often referred to as though they were monolithic entities with a single point of view. It is at best a simplification and in trying to understand developments at the EU level, it is less and less helpful to talk in this way. Rather the degree to which states – or in this instance national courts – act as unified, more-or-less monolithic systems, needs to be regarded as an open question. Nowhere has the significance of this been shown more clearly in discussing the relationship of the ECJ and national courts and legal systems, than in recent work by Anne-Marie Burley (now Slaughter) & Walter Mattli (Burley & Mattli, 1993; Mattli & Slaughter, 1996) and by Karen Alter (Alter, 1996). This has elucidated the process whereby European law has become accepted into national legal systems and their ideas will be briefly discussed here.

For Burley & Mattli (1993, p 63):

> *the entire process of increasing the use of the Article 177 procedure was an exercise in convincing national judges of the desirability of using the ECJ . . . [It was] designed to appeal to the self-interest primarily of the lower national courts. It succeeded ultimately in transforming the European legal system into a split system, in which these lower courts began to recognise two separate and distinct authorities above them.*

Alter develops this argument in terms of the realisation that different levels in national legal systems have different costs and benefits from any extension in the Court of Justice's authority. It is the higher courts generally that have had most to lose while lower courts found that their status and their powers could be enhanced by an application of EC law. Thus:

> *The different strategic calculations of national courts* vis-à-vis *the ECJ created a competition-between-courts dynamic of legal integration; this fed the process [of] legal integration and came to shift the national legal context from under high courts . . . [L]ower courts were the motor of EC legal integration into the national order, and legal expansion through their referrals to the ECJ.* (Alter, 1996, p 467)

This struggle can be seen in two distinct contexts. Astonishing as it may seem in the light of Article 177, which lays on courts, from which there is no appeal, the duty of referring any disputed question of EC law to the Court of Justice, the Constitutional Courts of no fewer than four of the original six signatories of the Treaty of Rome – Germany, Italy, Belgium and France – have never made such a referral! The way of avoiding such a referral is use of the *acte clair* doctrine, quite simply declaring that EC law is sufficiently transparent for no such referral to be necessary.

Lower courts have far fewer inhibitions. Not only, argues Alter, are they used to having their judgments rewritten or even overturned by higher courts, they are less concerned with the implications of individual judgments for the system as a whole. References to Europe allowed restrictive higher courts to be bypassed and for legal issues to be reopened:

> *Having an ECJ decision behind a lower-court decision also made its reversal by a higher court less likely. Thus, it actually bolstered the legal power and influence of the lower courts. For a lower court, the ECJ was akin to a second parent where parental approval wards off sanction.* (Alter, 1996, p 466)

Alter shows how higher courts tried but failed to stop lower courts making such reference. The Court of Justice played its part, too, in encouraging lower courts to make references to it. In a series of cases it tried to regulate the use of Article 177 generally in an open and permissive way. It has given a wide interpretation as to what constitutes a 'court' or 'tribunal' within the terms of Article 177, counting even arbitration bodies, as long as they have some sort of public authority backing, as qualified to make references. Thus in *Broekmeulen* (1981) the Dutch Appeals Committee for General Medicine with a third of its members appointed by the Dutch government was able to make a reference.

Similarly, the Court has ruled that the right to refer under Article 177 (2) is unfettered:

> *Any court or tribunal at any level is free, 'if it considers that a decision on the question is necessary to enable it to give judgment', to refer to the Court of Justice in any kind of proceedings.* (Steiner & Woods, 1996, p 394)

And, in *Rheinmühlen-Düsseldorf* (1974), the Court had ruled in the strongest possible terms that any court could refer to it whatever the provisions of national law. In other words, if a lower court felt that a superior court's judgment might force it to give a judgment contrary to Community law, its right to refer to Europe could not be countermanded by the superior court.

In *Simmenthal* (1979), already referred to in relation to the debate about supremacy, the Court was approached by an Italian judge wondering whether to wait for his own national constitutional court to declare invalid an Italian law which postdated (and contradicted) Article 30 of the Treaty. In its judgment the duty of the lower court to act on its own authority was unambiguously affirmed by the Court. The case is interesting not only in its own right but because it was the Italian Constitutional Court which had earlier attempted to stop references by lower courts to the ECJ, by arguing that all issues as to the validity of

European law were constitutional ones which it alone should decide. The ECJ judgment was, says Alter, '[a] direct challenge to the Italian Constitutional Court' (Alter, 1996, p 467).

While the right to make references is unfettered, the Court has allowed leeway to national courts in deciding when references are necessary to enable them to make a judgment. This obviously applies only to courts caught up in Article 177 (3) references (courts 'against whose decisions there is no judicial remedy under national law'). Under the *CILFIT* rules – laid down in *CILFIT* (1982) – referral was deemed unnecessary if the question of EC law was irrelevant, or – the Court's definition of *acte clair* – had either already been interpreted previously by the Court in similar circumstance or was a situation in which 'the correct application is so obvious as to leave no scope for reasonable doubt'.

This obviously allows a fair amount of room for interpretation and judges can in many cases, in all good faith and conscience, claim to be operating within the legitimate room for manoeuvre which the system provides. However political their desires may be, they have to be squared with legal doctrine that they themselves find acceptable. Even the situation with regard to supreme courts is not nearly as simple as perhaps suggested above with the reference to how Constitutional Courts have behaved. Other supreme courts in the countries mentioned have made Article 177 references; and the German Constitutional Court left its Bundesfinanzhof in no doubt that ignoring a Court ruling and failing to make an Article 177 reference was acting in breach of the Article 101 of the Basic Law, the German constitution – this in quelling a revolt in which the Finance Court had refused to accept the direct effect of a directive (Steiner & Woods, 1996, p 402).

By the late 1980s – over thirty years after the signing of the Treaty of Rome! – it seems finally to have become clear to national higher courts that the expansion of EC law could no longer be directly resisted. The *Nicolo* (1989) case, previously cited, in the French Conseil d'État is often taken to be the final point of resistance. There seems little doubt that pressure from below was instrumental in this process.

But it was not, as Burley & Mattli (1993) show, simply pressure from lower courts, no matter how significant this was. Their argument is a sophisticated rehabilitation of neo-functionalism, a theory developed in the 1950s and 1960s to account for the increasing integration of the Community which was then envisaged. As actors both above and below the nation state level pursued their self-interests in the nominally apolitical economic sphere, pressures, it was argued by neofunctionalists, would be generated which could lead to functional and eventually political 'spillover'.

What Burley & Mattli (1993, pp 57, 44) identify as 'the core insight of neo-functionalism – that integration is most likely to occur within a domain shielded from the interplay of direct political interests' is reaffirmed by them – but they see law replacing economics as this almost technical, non-political sphere. Their analysis is thus an account of how, in the nominally non-political domain of the law (in which '[l]aw functions as a mask for politics'), integration could proceed apace with forces above and below the state being generated and organised which had an interest in further integration.

In the first instance these forces were legal practitioners, law professors and lecturers as well as national court judges. The process is summed up well by Henry Schermers, EC legal academic and editor of the *Common Market Law Review*:

> *Much of the credit for the Community legal order rightly goes to the Court of Justice of the European Communities, but the Court will be the first to recognise that they do not deserve all the credit. Without the loyal support of*

*the national judiciaries, preliminary questions would not have been asked nor preliminary rulings followed. And the national judiciaries themselves would not have entered into Community law had not national advocates pleaded it before them. For the establishment and growth of the Community legal order it was essential for the whole legal profession to become acquainted with the new system and its requirements. Company lawyers, company solicitors and advocates had to be made aware of the opportunities offered to them by the Community legal system.* (Cited in Burley & Mattli, 1993, p 59)

On this level the empowerment of the Court 'simultaneously empowers all those who make their living analysing and critiquing its decisions' – creating an ever-expanding constituency of more-or-less loyal supporters even down to 'the recently created fifty seven new full-time teaching posts in community law' (Burley & Mattli, 1993, p 65).

Lest this theory seems too dependent on the self-interest of parties on the make, a more refined elaboration has been recently produced by the authors which draws on detailed country studies by scholars in Belgium, France, Germany, Great Britain, Italy and the Netherlands (Mattli & Slaughter, 1996, p 67). They show the process of reception to be a complex one in which such factors as particular legal cultures are also particularly important.

The process was caught well in its early stages by Scheingold. Looking at national courts' behaviour and evidence from interviews with attorneys etc he wrote in 1971 of 'the beginnings of consensual processes crystallising within and around the legal system':

*Of course, this development is somewhat erratic and the application of Community norms far from uniform. I would argue, however, that it is just this course of events which is likely to promote consensual patterns – that is to say, a process which softens rather than sharpens the hard edges of Community rules and thus makes them more palatable to all participants.* (Scheingold, 1965, p 46)

In this process Article 177 emerged, unexpectedly, as the main vehicle for advancing Community law. The Court had its origins in the European Coal and Steel Community (ECSC) with the clear role of policing the supra-national High Authority, not policing member-states' compliance. It was the High Authority (the forerunner of the Commission) which could do this unilaterally and could levy fines. Under the Treaty of Rome the Commission lost most of this power. If diplomacy failed, the Commission was now limited to proceeding against a member-state before the Court (Article 169). In the event of a breach all that was required was for the offending member 'to take the necessary measures to comply with the judgment of the Court' (Article 171). There were no sanctions. As well as the Commission initiating action, member states could also bring other member states' failure to comply before the Court (Article 170), but again, there were no sanctions. It seems certain that the main instruments for enforcing compliance were envisaged as the Commission (under Article 169) and the member states. Equally clearly, the powers of both of these were rather limited.

Article 177 was also taken over from the ECSC Treaty. There it seems to have been a mechanism of giving member states redress against invasive action due to lack of competence or infringement of an essential procedural requirement by any of the ECSC institutions (ECSC, Article 38). Quite why additional powers of interpretation were written in to it in the Treaty of Rome formulation is not clear, but there is real doubt as to whether the original Treaty drafters were aware of its potential. Alter (1996, p 484), for instance, writes that 'negotiators of the Treaty acknowledge that they had not imagined that national courts would use the preliminary ruling system to challenge the compatibility of national law with EC law.'

If Article 177's role in the Treaty framework remains unclear, however, its significance in reality is unquestioned. For it became the weapon the Court used so skilfully to give individual litigants a personal stake in EC law by allowing them to use it to challenge national law. Individuals were only to be given powers, however, to enhance community goals, not to undermine them. Individual empowerment was to be, as Burley & Mattli (1993, p 60) stress, a one-way ratchet mechanism. Under Article 173 individuals (together with Commission, Council and member states) were given powers to appeal to the Court to annul legal acts because they exceeded powers given under the Treaty. In one of the Court's earliest cases, *Plaumann* (1963), brought to it almost simultaneously with *Van Gend*, these powers were severely restricted.

In understanding all these developments, the Court has to be understood as a highly political actor, even if its justifications for its actions are generally in as non-political a language as possible. This, for Burley & Mattli, is crucial as well. The Court has presented itself as a bastion of pure legalism, simply spelling out the logic of what is inherent in the Treaties and secondary legislation. Aided until recently by the overwhelming mass of its interpreters – the number of critical voices is still relatively small – it has generally denied having any discretion or to be making policy at all. Shapiro (cited in Burley & Mattli, 1993, p 45) has satirised this well:

> *The Community [is presented] as a juristic idea; the written constitution as a sacred text; the professional commentary as a legal truth; the case law as the inevitable working out of the correct implications of the constitutional text and the constitutional court as the disembodied voice of right reason and constitutional teleology.*

The Court is not a political actor at all; it is 'merely' protecting the Community from ruin . . .

# 5

# The Court and Economic Integration

When discussing the reach of EC law, the question is largely posed in the form of the European Union versus the member states. Concern is often expressed over loss of sovereignty, national pride and the like. In turning to the Court and the economy, we are no longer really dealing with the same fault line. The issue is much less one of national economies versus the European economy, (though there are elements of this, to be sure) since in a fairly deep sense economic sovereignty has long been lost – not so much to the EU, but swamped rather by wider global processes. It is more a question of what is understood by free trade and the conditions required for its realisation, something that divides economic interests within member states. On top of this is the problem that economic analysis is never neutral. Categories like the 'economy', 'workers', 'migrants', 'distortion of competition' are ambiguous to their core. How they end up being defined is a highly political question with major social implications. This and the next chapter will explore some of the arguments which have unfolded in the Community over these issues: what kind of market is being constructed and therefore what kind of regulation is needed; also, since markets are always embedded in wider social structures and processes, who is gaining and who losing from those which have come to predominate in the Community, and how has the Court reacted, when faced with the need to make judgments (ie choices) in this area?

The European Economic Community was founded, precisely, as a Common Market: incorporating the shared external tariff barrier of a customs union together with the four freedoms listed in Article 3 EEC, viz free movement of goods, free movement of persons, freedom to provide services and free movement of capital; but much less than the federal union supporters of the deceased European Political Community had hoped for. The process was driven by the member states who combined together to preserve and strengthen their national interests. The Treaty of Rome was a bargain struck at a precise time and place. Inevitably, like all bargains, it contained a whole series of compromises and formulations pointing in somewhat different directions.

There is no such thing as unregulated capitalism; all kinds of interest groups want the economic system regulated, first and foremost, the large corporations. As Scheingold (1965, p 294) remarked in his study of the European Coal and Steel Community: 'It is perhaps an irony of economic integration that central intervention is necessary if a free market is to be established.' The real question always is, in whose interests regulation is structured and, insofar as the forms and patterns of regulation required shift over time, who controls the patterns of deregulation and reregulation which inevitably occur. Saying that the Treaty is cast in the language of free market liberalism, while true, tells little as to how it functions in practice.

To make sense of the framework within which the Treaty was cast requires reference to historical research and economic ideology, particularly that of Christian Democracy in Germany, then undergoing its 'economic miracle'. Far from wanting to implement free-market liberalism, there was among member states in the fifties, as Milward & Sørenson (Milward, Lynch et al, 1993, p 9) put it, 'a search for a new form of neo-mercantilist commercial policy which could combine a more rapid trade expansion with more selective and more easily adjustable forms of protection.' Chalmers (in Shaw & More, 1995, pp 55–72) has argued for the significance of a particular variety of economic philosophy developed in Germany, ordo-liberalism, which underpins the notion of the 'social market economy'. This recognises that economic systems have to be created, they cannot just be left to grow. It sees economic freedoms, however, as underpinning political ones so that the former, the market system freedoms, require constitutional protection. Furthermore, the market system is not the only economic order in society. Two such orders coexist within any society, complementary yet incompatible: a transaction order based on exchange and a centrally administered order based on direction. The implications of this are often expressed in the language of negative and positive integration – removal of restrictions in order to ensure the four market freedoms, and harmonisation, in order to ensure that certain socially determined standards are set and maintained. The idea that you can have one without the other, the single market with no attempt at harmonisation, was held perhaps by Margaret Thatcher, but by very few others. The dominant currents in continental thought have always wanted markets and regulation, encapsulated in the oft-repeated phrases about wanting 'level playing fields' and 'fair' rather than 'free' competition. The question is how (and in whose interests) such concepts are defined.

Regulation theorists have fruitfully analysed society by arguing that any successful 'regime of accumulation' has a corresponding 'mode of regulation'. The latter is necessary for the relatively smooth functioning of the former; it is, in effect, the set of social compromises which bind the various interests in society together via a more-or-less stable set of collective principles which can structure behaviour in society (see Lipietz, 1992, for an introduction to the ideas of regulation theory). There is, for instance, no simple day-to-day way in which the interests of finance capital and industrial capital coincide (witness the number of analyses of Britain's crisis in terms of the City versus manufacturing), let alone the interests of different nationally based capitals, or national vs multi-national capital. That is before other social interests are brought into the equation. Some social compromise has to be established if the system is to work at all, and there is no guarantee in advance that it will be a stable one.

The EU is perhaps best characterised as trying to develop an appropriate mode of regulation for what is a shifting, contradictory regime of accumulation – one moving rather half-heartedly from a set of stuttering, conflicting and cooperating national bases to a more clearly integrated European one. That, after all, is the overt project of economic integration. There is no clear and agreed meaning, however, on the nature and limits of integration to be achieved, and therefore of the kind and level of regulation required. Such regulation as exists at the EU level is a product of the Treaty and its development in secondary legislation. This, in turn, reflects the responses of both national and EU-wide forces to shifts in the global economy, to the vicissitudes of modern capitalism.

It is the Commission which is the institutional guardian of the economic goals of the Community, generally supported by the Court of Justice. For Ian Ward (1996a, p 118), what is apparent is 'the vigour of the ECJ in attempting to support the Commission in the effecting of the EC's economic policy', a policy very often constrained if not actually undermined by the actions of the Council, member states and corporate interests. I will look very briefly at the role of the ECJ in the spheres of competition policy and free movement of goods.

## COMPETITION POLICY

Competition policy is one of the few areas where the Commission has very wide powers under the Treaty – not only to initiate but also to make, implement and enforce policy. David Allen (1996b) talks of both the negative and the positive role of such policy. Negatively it merely polices the market by applying sanctions against those who abuse its freedoms. Positively, it is concerned with creating that market and the institutions and behaviour appropriate to it, a concern which can extend into wider economic, social and political areas. So, 'guided by the original treaties and supported by the Court of Justice in its rulings', DG IV (the competition directorate) has tried to extend free competition:

> *Nevertheless political and economic realities, as well as the practical problems of implementation, have often required DG IV either to turn a blind eye on uncompetitive practices, by both companies or member states, or to rationalise them in terms of other objectives being pursued by the Commission.* (Allen, 1996b, p 161)

The initial, negative integration emphasis of policy (removal of restrictions) in the 1960s gave way to an attempt to regulate the practices to which companies and member states increasingly turned in the economic recession of the 1970s.

There have been two major areas of concern for the Commission with regard to competition: control of mergers and control of state aids. There is, however, no specific mention of merger control in the Treaty, something which the Commission, rightly, saw as crucial in any competition policy. It tried, therefore, to fashion one out of creative interpretation of the Treaty, especially Articles 85 and 86 which dealt with rules of competition among private firms. Although Article 86 only allowed for action against firms abusing a dominant position (which might even be taken as suggesting that a dominant position was acceptable), the Commission used it in 1973 when it issued the *Continental Can* decision in which it argued that a dominant position was in itself an abuse.

When this came before the Court, the Commission interpretation of Article 86 was upheld, by linking it to the general competition objectives of Article 3(f) . 'This was,' affirms Allen (1996b, p 170), 'a classic example of the Court liberally interpreting the treaty in the interests of advancing supranational integration.' It was also an example of the Court rejecting the Commission's case on substantive grounds – allowing the merger to go ahead – while nonetheless ratifying the new principle it had sought to establish.

The Commission still wanted a firmer legal basis for merger control but failed to get any response to its 1973 regulation proposal from the Council of Ministers, until 1989! Many member states had their own merger control regimes and were reluctant to relinquish control to the Commission. Even with the move to the single market the politics of the situation were only swayed conclusively following a fortuitous Court ruling in the *Philip Morris* case (1987) where, 'against the then prevalent legal opinion' (Majone, 1996, p 272), Article 85(1) was interpreted as applying in principle to mergers. Again, an interventionist ruling from the Court transformed the situation. Given that the Commission now appeared to have its own relatively open-ended legal basis for approaching mergers, Council was stung into action in what might be termed an exercise in damage limitation. The 1989 Regulation on Mergers was the result, a consolidation but also a limitation of Commission powers.

The second major interference with free competition has been the question of state aid. Under Article 92 state aid which distorts the market is forbidden. Under Article 93 members states are required to notify the Commission of all existing and proposed state aids. This provision seems to have been more or less ignored by member states, so the Commission has relied on third parties making complaints which it can then investigate. In practice, not many cases were taken; but once again a Court decision came to the Commission's aid, curiously in another case involving Philip Morris in 1981, in which 'the Commission's right to exercise discretion "in the European interest" was firmly upheld by the Court ... the Court also seemed to be reminding the Commission of its obligations and responsibilities in this area' (Allen, 1996b, p 177). As a result the Court has clarified and developed its supervision of state aids, or at least those it comes to know about. State aids apparently account for between 10 and 20 per cent of public expenditure in member states, ie between 3 and 5 per cent of GDP according to Commission figures first collected in the late 1980s and confirmed in 1990s studies; contrast this with an EU budget which represents only 2.4 per cent of all public spending of member states and less than 1.3 per cent of EU GDP (Allen, 1996b, p 178; Majone, 1996, p 275).

## FREE MOVEMENT OF GOODS

The second area to consider, especially important in relation to the Court, is that of free movement of goods. This is covered by Articles 30–6 of the Treaty which deal with national barriers to trade and Articles 100, 100A and 100B which deal with the harmonisation of laws in this area.

According to Article 30: 'Quantitative restriction on imports and all measures having equivalent effect shall, without prejudice to the following provisions be prohibited between member states.' Article 36 nonetheless allows for restrictions on a variety of grounds including public morality, public policy or public security; the protection of health and life of humans, animals or plants; and the protection of national treasures' so long as they do not 'constitute a means of arbitrary discrimination or a disguised restriction on trade between member states'. The Court in its jurisprudence has traditionally been restrictive in its interpretation of the scope of this article (Armstrong, 1995, p 174). In the important *Dassonville* case

(1974) the Court was asked to rule on the Belgian state's demand that imported goods carry a certificate of origin issued by the state in which they were made. An importer of Scotch whisky from France had been unable to obtain such a certificate so had attached a home-made certificate to the goods – but found himself prosecuted for fraud. In what became known as the '*Dassonville* formula' the Court spelt out Article 30 so that:

> *All trading rules enacted by member states which are capable of hindering, directly or indirectly, actually or potentially, intra-Community trade are to be considered as measures having an effect equivalent to quantitative restrictions.*

It was not deemed necessary to show an actual hindrance to trade.

The effect of this was to widen greatly the scope of Community regulatory control.

> *Through the restriction of national regulatory compet-ence, the Court simultaneously asserted its own authority to review national regulatory measures while legitimating the Commission's role in the harmonisation of national laws.* (Armstrong, 1995, p 175)

In the deadlock of the 1970s, however, very little progress was made on harmonisation. It may have been in recognition of this that the Court gave its landmark ruling in the *Cassis de Dijon* (1979) case. Here the Court was asked to rule on the legality of a German law which required spirits to have a minimum alcohol content of 25 per cent, thus excluding French manufactured Cassis with its 15–20 per cent alcohol. The German government's public health and consumer protection justifications in the case were rejected, to nobody's surprise. The Court found 'no valid reason why, provided that they have been lawfully produced and marketed in one of the member states, alcoholic beverages should not be introduced into any other member state'. In what was by far the most important part of the judgment, it also enunciated the principle that certain state measures which fell within the *Dassonville* formula might nevertheless be acceptable if the restrictions they imposed on trade were 'reasonable'. Grounds included but were not limited to the effectiveness of fiscal supervision, protection of public health, fairness of commercial transactions and the defence of the consumer (Burrows, 1987, pp 57–61). National measures necessary to attain mandatory requirements would pass scrutiny so long as they were proportionate, but it would remain for the Court to supervise the regulatory space which it had now permitted to national governments.

The political reception of this judgment is interesting. It is widely but erroneously held to have introduced the principle of mutual recognition thus paving the way for the Single European Act and thus according the Court of Justice great powers in influencing the direction of the community. According to Martin Shapiro (1992, pp 129, 131), for example: '(T)he Court cut through the whole harmonisation and standard-setting tangle by establishing this principle of "mutual-recognition" . . . It is the Cassis approach to product standards that became the centre of the . . . 1992 process.' Alter & Meunier-Altsahalia's (1994) analysis of the case and its aftermath shows how wide of the mark this interpretation is. It is true that the Commission seized on the judgment and tried to extract a policy of mutual recognition from the judgment (which, incidentally, nowhere used that phrase). Quite simply, it failed. France, Germany and Italy in particular were strongly opposed and the Council's Legal Services interpreted the judgment differently. Indeed, subsequent Court judgments proved the critics right with the Court accepting as grounds for national rules, protection of culture (eg *Cinéthèque* (1985)) and environmental protection (*Commission* v *Denmark* (1988)). It also elaborated the rule of reason to allow for the requirement of 'functional equivalence' in *Commission* v *French Republic* (1986) where France was allowed to apply its own (higher) safety requirements to imported German woodworking machines on the grounds that they presumed a higher level of training than was prevalent in France (Alter & Meunier-Altsahalia, 1994, p 543). Nor did *Cassis* open the door to a floodgate of cases against national legislation – there were only 115 cases brought to the Court in the next ten years.

The Single European Act was in no sense a direct outcome of one part of a single Court judgment. It has to be seen in the context of falling European competitiveness internationally, the failure of nationally based policies in the 1970s and of a dramatically changed political environment reflected in political changes in Germany with the return of the CDU-FDP coalition, Britain in a return to the (now-Thatcherite) Tory party and France after Mitterrand's change of line in 1982–83. Despite all the actions of the Commission and the Court, non-tariff barriers in the early 1980s greatly exceeded those in existence at the end of the 1960s. It was this reality that underpinned the move to the single market.

The Court clearly favoured such a development; but it is a 'regulated single market' rather than a 'free market' which it has always done its best to foster. The drift of the choices the Court has made, evident in *Cassis* (1979) and after, are discussed further in the following chapter.

# 6

# The Narrow Economic Determination of the Project

It is clear that the Treaty framework and the majority of its concerns have been inspired by rather narrow economic conceptions. There are few clauses in the original treaties dealing with aspects of social or regional policy, for example. Their inspiration seems largely to have been out of fear that divergencies in these areas might lead to a 'distortion of competition'. Following Shaw (1996, pp 373–4), however, it might be better not to draw a sharp distinction between 'economic' and 'social' law in the Community, but to recognise that the central emphasis has been on issues concerned with the internal market rather than on those contingent to its development or which merely complement, or challenge, its development.

It is interesting, from this point of view, to take note of some areas where the Court seems to have gone out of its way to adopt an expansive and socially interventionist attitude, at least in certain phases: agriculture, employment protection and equal opportunities.

## AGRICULTURE

Agricultural support is a central concern of the Community, still taking more than half its total budget. What principles underpin this regulatory regime? Francis

Snyder (1990) uses an extremely interesting example of the sheepmeat regime in the Community, to draw out some general principles at work. He shows how quite different interpretations of the key Article 3(f) of the original Treaty, 'the institution of a system to ensure that competition in the common market is not distorted', are possible. There are, he affirms, two ideologies of competition which can be, and are, read into the unclear notion of 'distortion of competition'. In the first, the aim of the sheepmeat (or any other similar) regime is to 'permit, facilitate and encourage free intra-Community sheepmeat trade' and the support of farmers' incomes is a means to this objective. According to the second perspective, 'the primary purpose of the sheepmeat regime is to provide a legal framework for the negotiated adjustment of the very different market structures which currently coexist in the European Community's sheepmeat sector'; concern for 'the living conditions of a given region', in the words of an early EEC decision, are part of it (Snyder, 1990, pp 73–6).

From the first perspective, 'distortion of competition' simply means interference with free trade. From the second it means undue (ie unnegotiated) modification of existing structures. Although these two different approaches have often been associated with the national interests of Britain and France, the two main sheepmeat producers in the Community, Snyder is at pains to stress the variety of different, conflicting and often contradictory interests that exist. Large economic organisations, especially those closely linked to the import or export trade are more likely to favour the first perspective; medium farmers, marginal farmers, small and medium-sized wholesalers or retailers or processors, especially those associated with local farmers, are much more likely to favour the second (Snyder, 1990, pp 90–1).

The Court can also be seen at work in a number of interesting judgments in cases where EC legislation has been challenged as in violation of its own competition policy. In *Maizena* (1980) it allowed the setting of a quota for isoglucose production, despite the allegation that it breached the free access to an open market principle, on the grounds that agricultural policy took precedence over the Treaty's competition aims. In *Huiles usagées* (1985) it upheld a Council directive which provided for exclusive zones being assigned to waste oil collectors, arguing that while free trade was a fundamental right, there were 'inevitable restrictions which are justified by the pursuit of the objective of environmental protection which is in the general interest'. In Snyder's view assessing the jurisprudence as a whole,

> *it would be misleading to consider competition law to be the principal standard according to which the European Court evaluates – or should evaluate – the legal measures of the European Community's economic policy.* (1990, pp 95–6)

## ACQUIRED RIGHTS

The second 'interventionist' example is that of 'acquired rights'. These derive from Directive 77/187 which was concerned with safeguarding employees' rights in the events of takeovers and restructuring. This directive was originally part of the Social Action Programme and, in the words of Michael Shanks, EC Director General for social affairs at the time, aimed

> *to humanise the process of industrial change, on the basis that if this were not done the process of economic growth could itself be stopped by a backlash of social and political resistance.* (Cited in More, 1995, p 130)

The legal basis for the directive was Treaty Article 100, ie it was grounded on the Treaty concern to eliminate 'distortions of competition' in a common market, in this case the unfair advantage that a company in one member state might have over another if it could cut labour costs more than a company in another member state by getting rid of workers.

The rights protected are minimum ones. Where there is a 'transfer of undertakings', employees continue to be employed on the same terms and conditions as before. The protection is only on transfer and not for the long-term, and dismissals for 'economic, technical or organis-ational reasons entailing changes in the workforce' (Article 4(1)) are excluded. As More (1995, p 132) demonstrates, however, the Court's interpretation of what a transfer is

> *has consistently been in keeping with its aim of employment protection and its origins in the Social Action Programme, holding that the directive is applicable to the protection of the rights of employees in an ever-wider range of situations.*

For example, in *Rask* (1992) the contracting out of canteen services by Phillips was held to be a 'legal transfer'. In *Schmidt* (1994) a 'bare contract for service' was deemed sufficient, there being no need for a transfer of assets.

There is no doubt that such interpretation is at variance with the more extreme deregulatory policies pursued, for example, by the last Conservative government in Britain with its assault on in-house local service provision. For many years there has also been intense political pressure, from Germany and Britain in particular, to rewrite the directive to increase the flexibility which firms have in relation to their labour force. That is a mammoth task in that unanimity would be required for the adoption of a revised directive; nonetheless the Commission tried, without success, to do just that in 1994. Despite its failure, with the increasing emphasis on employment creation and flexibility in the Community (especially in the

Commission's 1993 *White Paper*), there is now some evidence of a Court response and a restriction of the wide protection it had been prepared to confer on employees.

In *Süzen* [1997] which seems to be a reversal of *Schmidt*, it was held that 'the directive did not apply to a situation in which a person who had entrusted the cleaning of his premises to a first undertaking terminates his contract with the latter and, for the performance of similar work, enters into a new contract with a second undertaking' if there is no transfer of significant assets or the taking over of 'a major part of the workforce' by the second company. (See the discussion in Hunt, 1997)

## EQUAL OPPORTUNITIES

The third area to be looked at briefly is that of equal opportunities based on Article 119 and directives associated with it. It highlights well the ambiguous nature of the relationship of the economic to the social in the EU, down to the fact that what became Article 119 was shifted from the economic core of the Treaty from a section dealing with distortions of competition, to a Title on social policy during the Treaty negotiations (Hoskyns, 1996, pp 42, 57).

Article 119 wrote the bare principle of equal pay for equal work into the Treaty to satisfy French demands. It lay more or less in limbo until *Defrenne (2)* in 1974, previously mentioned, which recognised its direct effect. Soon however, as part of the reforming movement of the early 1970s the Court had three directives, concerning equal pay, equal treatment and social security, to guide it. Two more were to follow, in very different political circumstances in the mid-80s, concerning equal treatment in occupational pension schemes and self-employment. As a result of these, and subsequent Court litigation, much of it brought by the British and Northern Irish Equal Opportunities Commissions, a number of real gains were consolidated: for example, equality in retirement age, occupational pension age, redundancy and *ex gratia* payments and an expectation of effective remedy when discrimination has been established.

Thus in certain areas of employment rights and equal opportunities, the Court seems to have taken the view that a stronger social dimension has to be defended than many member states would like. The Court's judgments, however, especially in the equal opportunities arena, also show severe limitations. The most extensive analysis of the history of women and law in the EU is Catherine Hoskyns's *Integrating Gender*. According to her,

> *improving the situation of women has never been a prime objective of the Court, and . . . its rulings only have that effect if the interest of women coincide with other objectives being pursued.* (1996, p 159)

Thus rulings relating to employment issues have tended to be supportive and have even resulted in expansive Court judgments. Those relating to social security, which most easily cross over into family and dependency issues have seen the Court's judgments becoming 'steadily more minimalist'. This line of interpretation was also in tune, as Hoskyns points out, with Delors's own policy preferences and the general 'intellectual context' of the times, keen for a wider social dimension than the Council would in fact agree to, but not envisaging a place for such things as individualising benefits, attacking women's dependency on men, or valuing domestic labour. (Hoskyns, 1996, pp 160, 161)

This restrictive view can be seen even more clearly when one looks at the discriminatory effect of the law in defining what are indeed central concepts like 'worker' and 'family'. (For a general discussion see Hervey (1995) and Ward (1996b)). Despite the rhetoric of level playing fields, concern does not extend so far as the broad interests of marginalised and peripheral groups including a wide category of women and members of ethnic minorities. In Tamara Hervey's words: 'The all-pervasive concept of the "market" is one mechanism by which this marginalisation may be achieved' (1995, p 93). In her analysis:

> *The function of the Community market ideology seems to be to determine* precisely which *interests are to be promoted in the name of the market. It is this market ideology, not simply free competition, which informs, for example, the (directly or indirectly) racially discriminatory construct of 'European' which in turn defines 'migrant worker' and 'family' in the context of Community law.*
> (Hervey, 1995, p 109)

The Court has not helped. The term 'migrant worker', a category protected from any discrimination on the grounds of nationality in Treaty Article 6, has been relatively generously construed by the Court, but only with regard to European Union nationals (and even here there are reservations, discussed below). The legitimate Third Country nationals (ie people from non-EU countries) within the EU (possibly 10 million in total) are not covered, though any Court wishing to have made a broad judgment would be aided by Article 48(1) which states simply that 'Freedom of movement for workers shall be secured within the Community by the end of the transitional period [ie 1968] at the latest.' Similarly with regard to family members there is a hierarchy of entitlement to benefit: fullest entitlements for families of European Union nationals migrant workers; lesser benefits for families of other European Union nationals with residence rights only if the entire family is covered by health insurance; and no benefits whatsoever for families of Third Country nationals outside the member state in which they reside. The fact that about 70 per cent of Third Country nationals are members of ethnic minorities means that the lesser treatment of them will also have racist effects (Hervey, 1995, p 109).

The racist element of the entire European Union enterprise is reinforced by the developments of the Schengen Convention, now involving some eleven of the member states. Established notionally to facilitate free movement by the removal of internal border controls, it has developed a veritable obsession with border controls, restricting asylum rights and exclusion generally. It sets the tone for wider discussions within the EU, which now fall under the third pillar, Justice and Home Affairs. Free movement may be one of the fundamental rights established by the Treaty of Rome, but where aliens are concerned, it is more or less equated with crime, drugs trafficking and illegal immigration. As there is a presumption that any visible 'foreigner' is an illegal immigrant, many members of ethnic communities including European Union nationals, find they are *de facto* objects of suspicion. All of this, while not involving the Court directly, creates an atmosphere of hostility and fear, contributing to a restrictive and ungenerous social climate. In associated areas where it does have jurisdiction and could make a difference, the Court has not exactly rushed to do so. It is worth contrasting the Court's much-vaunted interventionism with its caution, if not pusillanimity, towards the rights of the most disadvantaged members of the Community who are, in the title of Ian Ward's (1996b) book, on 'the margins of European law'.

The remark that the Court has generally construed the meaning of the term migrant worker broadly needs qualifying, even in relation to EU nationals. In a series of cases the Court has established that such workers still have to undertake work which is an 'effective and genuine economic activity', not one which is 'marginal and ancillary' (see Hervey, 1995, p 104 for a list of cases). Caring for dependants and unpaid household work generally is not valued, with obvious gender implications, complementing those discussed above with regard to the failure of the Court in employment-related issues. Similarly, if you want to claim protection of the law you have to live in the right kind of family. Two well-known cases are worth citing. In *Netherlands* v *Reed* (1986) the Court rejected a definition of 'spouse' which would have included unmarried couples in stable cohabiting relationships; and the effect of *Diatta* v *Land Berlin* (1985) was that the Third Country national wife of an EU national husband, formally separated, would be subject to deportation on the annulment of the marriage. On the issues on which the women's movement has been campaigning for nearly thirty years – child-care provisions, protection of atypical workers, recognition of flexible career patterns etc – the Court has generally stood aside (Hervey, 1995; Ward, 1996b).

The way in which key concepts are constructed by Community legislation is incisively revealed in Joanne Scott's (1995) study of Community regional policy. Development of 'lagging regions' is defined, in wholly quantifiable GDP terms, synonymously with growth. Commodification is its watchword, applied, also, to the environment which is largely valued for the economic benefits it can bring, for example as a tourist resource. An alternative and much richer language of need, entitlement and indeed self-determination is effectively eliminated. International law, particularly that encapsulated in resolutions of the General Assembly of the United Nations, one of the few international institutions to provide space for Third World voices, is, Scott argues, much more advanced. It has declared a new human right, a right to development and sees 'the human person (as) the central subject of development and . . . the active participant and beneficiary of the right to development' (UN Declaration on the Right to Development cited in Scott, 1995, p 68). Moreover, it is centrally concerned with the distribution of wealth and benefits that derive from development as well as with the protection of human rights (Scott, 1995, pp 66–9). Scott stresses the marginalisation of the moment of positive integration in the move to a single market. The substance of her critique makes it clear that even positive integration on a narrowly market-oriented base would still be socially highly discriminatory.

What is needed is an altogether more expansive and generous basis for European integration than we have in the Treaty of Rome and its various amendments. Such changes would obviously also affect the role of the ECJ. These arguments are elaborated in the conclusion below.

# 7

# Towards a New Role for the Court of Justice in a Democratic European Union?

The burden of the previous analysis can be summed up in a few propositions. The Court has clearly been interventionist is some arenas and directions and rather cautious in others. To admire, or condemn, its activism and creativity only tells part of the story; as important has been its unwillingness to be active or creative in other circumstances. What accounts for the differences in its responses in different arenas?

The areas of maximum creativity are largely related to those concerned with 'constitutionalisation' of the Treaties. Commentators generally seem to express great admiration for the Court in this process, keeping alive the Community ideal in difficult times. A more sceptical interpretation might also note how such high-minded idealism happened to coincide with the Court's interests in consolidating its own power and prestige.

Whatever the gloss one puts on this development, however, there seems little doubt that the Court has, over time, been quite a subtle political actor. It has occasionally stirred the waters with its judgments, but has also been willing to modify and adjust the emphasis of its jurisprudence in many areas in response to its reception and the wider political and social climate among elite groups in the Community.

Generally, but by no means always, the Court's judgments are in line with the views of the Commission.
Without suggesting any collusion, it might nonetheless be
helpful to see the Court and the Commission in a double
act – the Court able to push out the boat of integration
and step on toes in the process in ways the Commission
could never dare to do. Indeed many Article 177 references have come from the Court on issues which the
Commission has refused to handle or simply failed to
progress.

Finally, the Court's judgments are not generally arbitrary. Unexpected at times, certainly, and quite possibly
over-reaching, but they are comprehensible in terms of a
commitment to a certain kind of European Community,
to a certain kind of economic integration. As the previous
section has argued, it is a market-led integration, an
integration in which the economic subsumes the social,
the environmental, the political. The latter do not
disappear, except in extreme and unworkable free market
models. Even within the framework of market-led integration there are substantive choices to be made and the
Court has at times upheld social, environmental or other
rights if these are seen as contributing to the wider goal.
Experience, however, suggests there are strict limits as to
how far the Court will go in this direction.

Earlier in this paper, the question as to how faithful the
Court has been to the intentions of the 'founding fathers'
was raised. For even as convinced an intergovernmentalist
as Andrew Moravcsik:

> *The decisions of the Court clearly transcend what
> was initially foreseen and desired by most national
> governments. The 'Constitutionalisation' of the Treaty
> of Rome was unexpected. It is impossible, moreover, to
> argue that the current system is the one to which all
> national governments would currently consent, as recent
> explicit limitations on the Court in the Maastricht Treaty
> demonstrate.* (Cited in Pierson, 1996, p 134)

How, then, did a situation come about in which the Court has as much autonomy as it appears to have? A thorough-going and convincing account is given in the approach of historical institutionalism, expounded most notably by Paul Pierson (1996). In brief, supranational institutions are given some autonomy by the states that set them up since they could not otherwise function to fulfil the goals they are established to achieve in the first place. These institutions can and do use their resources to increase their own power and there is clearly much evidence of the Commission and the Court doing precisely this.

However, and this is the nub of the analysis, the states which have ceded some of their authority to these joint institutions find they cannot simply bend these to their will. Pierson offers a convincing account both as to why gaps will emerge between the long-term interests of the member states and of the institutions they have created; and why they can be difficult if not impossible to close.

Gaps emerge, importantly, from the unanticipated consequences of political action, especially in a body like the EU characterised by 'high issue density' (Pierson, 1996, p 137), which cuts across almost all domestic issues. This leads to problems of overload – time, expertise, scarcity of information etc – as well as spillover, the inability to isolate one sector from another. In addition there is the logic of electoral politics. Politicians have short time horizons, while those of the institutions created can be a good deal longer. Furthermore, preferences shift in response to changing circumstances and governments can and do change.

The idea that once gaps are identified they can easily be closed may be justified in a highly competitive market environment if one, unsatisfactory, supranational regime could be simply replaced by another or coerced into line by the threat of replacement. At the European level, however, there are no alternative regimes waiting in the wings. The EU, indeed, has proved more resilient than the competing economic regimes of Comecon or the

European Free Trade Association (EFTA). It not only survives but is the only supranational pole of attraction, a beacon to all non-member states in Europe. Short of exit, which no country is seriously contemplating, member states are reduced to having to work within an environment beyond their individual or even collective control.

The EU was endowed with considerable resources at its creation. As Pierson (1996, p 143) puts it, because they cannot have continuous control over new institutions they create, designers 'must consider the likelihood that future governments will be eager to overthrow their designs, or to turn the institutions they create to other purposes'. Structures were created that the individual member states were not able to control, precisely to stop other member states or future governments defecting from them. 'In shutting out their potential successors, Chiefs of Government have indeed shut themselves out as well' (Pierson, 1996, p 144).

This is clear, for example, in the emergence of policy innovation at the European level. The simple view that harmonisation would mean least common denominator solutions is not borne out in practice, especially post-Single European Act (SEA). According to Majone (1996, p 266), 'a number of directives in the area of social regulation – environmental protection, consumer protection, health and safety at the workplace – represent significant innovations with respect to the policies of most member states', a process which he has analysed at length.

The unanimity required for Treaty reform makes it extraordinarily difficult to assemble a coalition for changing the fundamental architecture of the Union. That does not mean that member states do not try, individually and collectively, to evade the consequences of their own creations. Joseph Weiler's (1991) account of the stages of this process is compelling. In response to developments of legal supranationalism in the 1960s, he argues that, in 'what may be almost termed a ruthless process, member states took control over Community decisionmaking'

(Weiler, 1991, p 2423). In the process we see familiar land-marks like the Luxembourg Accord, Coreper and the establishment of the European Council.

From 1973 to the mid eighties, the pattern shifts. The restricted nature of the competences transferred to the Community (the pooling of sovereignties 'albeit in limited fields') began to be eroded, so that no core of state powers was beyond Community reach. This growth of powers 'willed by all actors involved', was often predicated on the 'elastic' Article 235 which became more broadly inter-preted, by all parties concerned, than originally intended, when it was merely to allow a legal basis for activities necessary to attain the limited joint objectives of the Treaty already explicitly agreed, but where no explicit powers had been granted.

> *[T]his wide reading, in which all political institutions partook, meant that it would become virtually impossible to find an activity which could not be brought within the 'objectives of the Treaty'.* (Weiler, 1991, pp 2435, 2445–6)

A Community without limit to its competences was not what member states had signed up to, as political oppos-itionists of all colours have not been slow to point out – nor, indeed, have the supreme and/or constitutional courts in various member states. This was not a problem when decisions were made under 'the shadow of the veto': following the introduction of Qualified Majority Voting, however, they are now made 'under the shadow of the vote' (Weiler, 1991, pp 2461–2). Issues of the legitimacy of the whole construction, buried while member states had veto control, have surfaced once more.

In other words, while member states might object very strongly to particular Court decisions the process as a whole was one in which the executive branch of government prospered, together with the judicial, at both member state and European level. This does not mean there is no conflict between executive and judiciary or between the executive at national level and at European level. Quite the reverse. The latter conflict has often been quite extreme as shown clearly by the behaviour of Britain under the Conservatives (and to some extent continued under Labour). The ongoing refusal of member states' courts to accept supremacy on the Court's terms is a marker that this struggle is by no means over.

There has been little attempt to roll back the Court, however, more an effort to contain it. Where Treaty revision at Maastricht brought new areas of competence into the Union, as opposed to the Community, in the second and third pillars, member states were quite explicit in excluding the Court from having any jurisdiction. Its powers in the areas over which it had clear jurisdiction were, if anything, enhanced at Maastricht. Article 171 was amended to allow the Court to fine defaulting member states, greatly enhancing the power of the Union over its constituent members.

The big loser in this whole process has been democracy. As competences expanded, national parliaments were increasingly bypassed. Interest groups mobilised at the national level also found themselves marginalised. The democratic deficit is not a contingent feature of the history of the European Union. It is structured into its very foundations. Member states have been extremely reluctant to increase the powers of the European Parliament – in the UK's case, clearly in order to maintain the strong executive powers which characterise the political system, in the case of countries like Denmark or Sweden, in order to prevent their national democracies and national parliaments from being further undermined. Neither approach, unfortunately, contributes much to democracy at Union level. The need for fundamental constitutional reform in the EU is urgent, for a genuine constitutional-isation process in place of the behind-the-backs-of-the-citizenry process that has taken place to date, in which 'judicialisation' has been equated with 'constitutional-isation' (Kuper, 1998a).

The role of law in such a genuinely democratic society is important in maintaining the conditions which enable democracy to exist at all. It should not seek to be a substitute arena for the balancing of interests, which is the proper role of the democratic process in a democratic society. A European Court of Justice will of course play an important part in any democratic, decentralised, socially and environmentally aware future construction of Europe. One of its chief roles would be to safeguard and enhance individual and collective rights, rights that derive from a consideration of citizens' needs and human-itarian considerations, not from the abstract needs of the market. The Court bears some of the blame for not having delivered these to date – but only some, given the political climate and lack of vision on which Europe is currently based (on rights in the EU generally see de Búrca, 1993; Coppel & O'Neill, 1992; Lenaerts, 1991; Twomey, 1994; Weiler & Lockhart, 1995). Such rights can only be fully realised in a genuinely participatory and democratised political process at all levels – local, regional, national and European. Lest the Europe that emerges has any fortress characteristics, let it be stressed from the outset that the idea of Europe described above cannot be built nor can it survive in splendid isolation, excluding both at its frontiers and within the poor, the persecuted and the oppressed.

A Court dedicated to seeing that people get the rights that are due to them would need to be much more welcoming to those groups in society who, in practice, are currently least likely or able to use it. There is some room even now to use the Court as one weapon in the armoury to further the interests of marginalised groups. The Equal Opportunities Commission's 'litigation strategy' (not what it started out as, but what it became) (Barnard, 1995, pp 253–72) shows some of the potential of this approach – but also its limitations (Hoskyns, 1996).

Perhaps there is mileage in Scott's suggestion of trying to challenge the legitimacy of Community law in the context of regional development. After all, the Court has recognised that rights in the Community have to be drawn from 'international treaties for the protection of human rights on which the member states have collaborated or of which they are signatories'. All experience suggests, however, that it is the wider distribution of power in society that will determine who has access to and benefits from the legal system in general. It was large retailers in Britain who used Article 177 references in order to challenge the Sunday trading laws. In doing so they were part of a European-wide strategy, with corporate interests elsewhere involved (Rawlings cited in Mattli & Slaughter, 1996, p 6). Just as it was French corporate import and export interests who led a sustained attack on the Conseil d'État in the later 1980s, bringing about its *Nicolo* (1989) change of heart (Plötner cited in Mattli & Slaughter, 1996, p 6). So many Article 177 references which have established economic, commercial and property rights or rights of the defence have been applications made by companies in the latter category often in opposition to the Commission's use of its investigative powers (de Búrca, 1995, p 32).

Stephen Sedley (now Justice Sedley), writing in a different context, contrasted what free speech means for different actors: for Rupert Murdoch the right to print what he likes, for those traduced by him an enforceable right of reply. In response to a US Supreme Court ruling that Murdoch's was the dominant right Sedley (1991, p 5) comments:

> *If we disagree, as we should with [this outcome], it is not because of a difference of legal reasoning but because of a difference of social and political goals . . . the very neutrality with which laws are applied can be an instrument of oppression in a society governed by market principles.*

Burley and Slaughter (Mattli, 1996, p 13), trying to understand how judges operate in liberal democracies, identify two constraints on them: 'a minimum fidelity to the demands of legal discourse' and a 'minimum democratic accountability: the requirement that a court not stray too far from majority political preferences'. The problem of course is how the latter are divined. In a radically inegalitarian society, not all voices are equal. Judges by habit, temperament and training are not instinctively radical. What pass for majority political preferences are generally those of certain elites, assiduously fostered by the media conglomerates.

In a discussion of democracy and the Court of Justice, Mancini and Keeling (1994, p 183) write that:

> The effect of Van Gend en Loos was to take Community law out of the hands of politicians and bureaucrats and to give it to the people. Of all the Court's democratising achievements none can rank so highly in practical terms.

It is wrong on both counts. The 'people' who benefit from the internal market and its Court are not all the people within the European Union; nor are they all the people of Europe. To equate an individual's right to litigate with democracy is to narrow the concept appallingly. Democracy, if it is to be anything, will empower the millions and millions of citizens of Europe in the collective construction of their own political, social, economic and environmental reality, not largely in their individual rights of redress against injustice, no matter how important these are. There is a long way to go.

In the absence of a political climate and the mobilisation of wide interests favouring such changes, the effects of which has penetrated into the Commission itself, there is unlikely to be a favourable outcome from the Court. Or, to put it another way, it is possible that the Court can be used as one arm in a campaign for wider democratisation and human rights. It is the campaign itself, however, which will be crucial.

# CASED CITED

# European Court of Justice Cases

*Broekmeulen* v *Huisarts Registratie Commissie*, (1981) case
246/80

*Cassis de Dijon: Rewe Zentrale AG* v *Bundesmonopolver-
waltung für Branntwein*, (1979) case 120/78

*CILFIT* (1982) case 283/81

*Cinéthèque* v *Fédération Nationale des Cinémas Français*,
(1985) cases 60-61/84

*Commission* v *Denmark*, (1988) (re disposable beer cans)
case 302/86

*Commission* v *French Republic*, (1986) case 188/84

*Continental Can: Europemballage Corp and Continental
Can Inc* v *Commission*, (1973) case 6/72

*Costa* v *Ente Nazionale per l'Energia Elettrica (ENEL)*, (1964)
case 6/64

*Dassonville: Procureur du Roi* v *Dassonville*, (1974) case
8/74

*Defrenne* v *SA Belge de Navigation Aérienne*, SABENA, No 2
(1976) case 43/75

*Diatta* v *Land Berlin*, (1985) case 267/83

*ERTA: Commission* v *Council*, (1971) case 22/70

*Faccini Dori* v *Recreb Srl*, (1994) case C 91/92

*Factortame: Firma Brasseries du Pecheur* v *Germany* and *R* v
*Secretary of State for Transport, ex parte Factortame Ltd*,
(1993) (Factortame 3), Joined cases C 46 & 48/93

*Francovich* v *Italy*, (1991) cases C 6&9/90

*Franz Grad* v *Finanzamt Traunstein*, (1970) case 9/70
*Huiles usagées: Procureur de la République* v *Association de défense des bruleurs de huiles usagées*, (1985) case 240/83
*Internationale Handelsgesellschaft mbH* (1970) case 11/70
*Kolpinguis Nijmegen* (1987) case 80/86
*Les Verts: Parti Ecologiste Les Verts* v *European Parliament*, (1986) case 294/83
*Maizena GmbH* v *Council of the European Communities* (1980) case 139/79
*Marleasing SA* v *La Comercial Internacional de Alimentación SA*, (1990) case C 106/89
*Marshall* v *Southampton & South West Hampshire Area Health Authority (Teaching)*, (1986) case 152/84
*Netherlands* v *Reed*, (1986) case 59/85
*Nold: J Nold KG* v *Commission*, (1974) case 4/73
*Plaumann & Co* v *Commission*, (1963) case 25/62
*Rask* v *ISS Kantineservice A/S*, (1992) case C 209/91
*Rheinmühlen-Düsseldorf* v *Einfuhr- und Vorratsstelle für Getreide und Futtermittel (No 1)*, (1974) case 166/73
*Schmidt* v *Spar- und Leihkasse der früheren Ämter Bordesholm, Kiel und Cronshagen*, (1994) case C 392/92
*Simmenthal SpA* v *Commission*, (1979) case 92/78
*Stauder* v *City of Ulm*, (1969) case 29/69
*Süzen* v *Zehnecker Gebäudereinigung*, (1997) case C 13/95
*Van Duyn* v *Home Office*, (1974) case 41/74
*Van Gend: NY Algemene Transport- en Expeditie Onderneming Van Gend en Loos* v *Nederlandse Administratie der Belastingen*, (1963) case 26/62
*Von Colson* v *Land Nordrhein-Westphalen*, (1984) case 14/83
*Walgrave and Koch* v *Association Union Cycliste Internationale*, (1974) case 36/74

# French Cases

*Boisdet* (Conseil d'État, 24 September 1990)
*Cohn-Bendit* (Conseil d'État, 22 December 1978)
*Compagnie Générale des Eaux* (Conseil d'État, 23 July 1993)
*Nicolo* (Conseil d'État, 20 October 1989)
*Rothmans* and *Philip Morris* (the *Cigarette Cases*): *Société Arizona Tobacco Products* and *Philip Morris France*, 28 February 1992)
*Société des Cafés Jacques Vabre (Cours de Cassation, 24 May 1975)*

# Acronyms and Abbreviations

EC     European Community
ECJ    European Court of Justice
ECSC  European Coal and Steel Community
EEC   European Economic Community
EFTA  European Free Trade Association
EU     European Union
SEA   Single European Act

# References

Allen David (1996a) 'Cohesion and structural adjustment', in Helen Wallace & William Wallace (eds), *Policy-Making in the European Union*, 3rd revised, Oxford: Oxford University Press, pp. 209–34

Allen David (1996b) 'Ch 6: Competition policy', in Helen Wallace & William Wallace (eds), *Policy-Making in the European Union*, 3rd revised, Oxford: Oxford University Press, pp. 157–83

Alter Karen J. (1996/July) 'The European Court's political power', *West European Politics*, 19(3), pp. 458–87

Alter Karen & Meunier-Aitsahalia Sophie (1994/Jan) 'Judicial politics in the European Community: European integration and the pathbreaking *Cassis de Dijon* decision', *Comparative Political Studies*, 26(4), pp. 535–61

Armstrong Kenneth (1995) 'Regulating the free movement of goods: institutions and institutional change', in Jo Shaw & Gillian More (eds), *New Legal Dynamics of European Union*, Oxford: Clarendon Press, pp. 165–91

Bainbridge Timothy with Teasdale Anthony (1995) *The Penguin Companion to European Union*, London: Penguin

Barnard Catherine (1995) 'A European litigation strategy: the case of the Equal Opportunities Commission', in Jo Shaw & Gillian More (eds), *New Legal Dynamics of European Union*, Oxford: Clarendon Press, pp. 253–72

Barnard C. & Sharpson E. (1997) 'The changing face of Article 177 references', *Common Market Law Review,* 34, pp. 1113–71

de Búrca Gráinne (1993) 'Fundamental human rights and the reach of EC law', *Oxford Journal of Legal Studies,* 13(3), pp. 283–319

de Búrca Gráinne (1995) 'The language of rights and European integration', in Jo Shaw & Gillian More (eds), *New Legal Dynamics of European Union,* Oxford: Clarendon Press, pp. 29–54

Burley Anne-Marie & Mattli Walter (1993/Winter) 'Europe before the Court: a political theory of legal integration', *International Organization,* 47(1), pp. 41–76

Burrows F. (1987) *Free Movement in European Community Law,* Oxford: Clarendon Press

Bzdera André (1992/July) 'The Court of Justice of the European Community and the politics of institutional reform', *West European Politics,* 15(2), pp. 122–36

Chalmers Damien (1995) 'The single market: from prima donna to journeyman', in Jo Shaw & Gillian More (eds), *New Legal Dynamics of European Union,* Oxford: Clarendon Press, pp. 55–72

Closa Carlos (1994) 'Citizenship of the Union and nationality of member states', in David O'Keefe & Patrick M. Twomey (eds), *Legal Issues of the Maastricht Treaty,* London: Chancery Law Publishing, pp. 109–19

Coppel Jason & O'Neill Aidan (1992) 'The European Court of Justice: taking rights seriously', *Legal Studies,* 12, pp. 227–45

Craig P.P. (1992) 'Once upon a time in the west: direct effect and the federalisation of EEC law', *Oxford Journal of Legal Studies,* 12(4), pp. 453–79

Docksey Chris (1991/Dec) 'The principle of equality between women and men as a fundamental right under Community law', *Industrial Law Journal,* 20(4), pp. 258–80

Everson Michelle (1995) 'The legacy of the market citizen', in Jo Shaw & Gillian More (eds), *New Legal Dynamics of European Union*, Oxford: Clarendon Press, pp. 73–90

Gustavsson Sverker (1998) 'Defending the democratic deficit' in Albert Weale & Michael Nentwich, (eds), *The Political Theory of European Constitutional Choice*, London: Routledge, forthcoming

Hartley T.H. (1994) *The Foundations of EC Law*, Oxford: Clarendon Press

Hervey Tamara (1994) 'Legal issues concerning the *Barber* protocol', in David O'Keefe & Patrick M. Twomey (eds), *Legal Issues of the Maastricht Treaty*, London: Chancery Law Publishing, pp. 329–37

Hervey Tamara (1995) 'Migrant workers and their families in the European Union: the pervasive market ideology of Community law', in Jo Shaw & Gillian More (eds), *New Legal Dynamics of European Union*, Oxford: Clarendon Press, pp. 91–110

Hoskyns Catherine (1996) *Integrating Gender: Women, Law and Politics in the European Union*, London: Verso

Hunt Jo (1997) 'The Court of Justice as a policy actor in the development of the EC Labour Law regime: the case of the acquired rights directive', Conference Paper, Second UACES Research Conference, Loughborough

Kuper Richard (1998a) 'The making of a constitution for Europe', *Contemporary Politics*

Kuper Richard (1998) 'The many democratic deficits of the European Union' in Albert Weale & Michael Nentwich, (eds), *The Political Theory of European Constitutional Choice*, London: Routledge, forthcoming

Lecourt Robert (1976) *L'Europe des Juges*, Bruxelles: Emile Bruylant

Lenaerts Koen (1991/Oct) 'Fundamental rights to be included in a Community catalogue', *European Law Review*, 16, pp. 367–90

Lipietz Alain (1993) 'Social Europe, legitimate Europe: the inner and outer boundaries of Europe', *Environment and Planning D*, 11, pp. 501–12

Lipietz Alain (1992) *Towards a New Economic Order*, Cambridge: Polity

MacCormick Neil (1993/Jan) 'Beyond the sovereign state', *Modern Law Review*, 56(1), pp. 1–18

Majone Giandomenico (1996) 'Ch 15: A European regulatory state?', in Jeremy Richardson (ed.), *European Union: Power and Policymaking*, London: Routledge, pp. 263–77

Mancini G. Federico (1991) 'The making of a constitution for Europe', in Robert O Keohane & Stanley Hoffman (eds), *The New European Community*, Boulder, Colorado: Westview Press, pp. 177–94

Mancini G. Federico & Keeling David T. (1994/Mar) 'Democracy and the European Court of Justice', *Modern Law Review*, 57(2), pp.175–90

Mattli Walter & Slaughter Anne-Marie (1996) 'Constructing the European Community legal system from the ground up: the role of individual litigants national courts', *Harvard Jean Monnet Chair Working Paper Series*, Paper 6/96

Milward Alan S. (1993) *The European Rescue of the Nation-State*, London: Routledge

Milward Alan S., Lynch Frances M.B., et al (1993) *The Frontier of National Sovereignty: History and Theory 1945–1992*, London: Routledge

More Gillian (1995) 'The Acquired Rights Directive: frustrating or facilitating labour market flexibility', in Jo Shaw & Gillian More (eds), *New Legal Dynamics of European Union*, Oxford: Clarendon Press, pp. 129–45

Newman Michael (1996) *Democracy, Sovereignty and the European Union*, London: Hurst

O'Keefe David (1992/Feb) 'The free movement of persons and the single market', *European Law Review*, 17, pp. 3–19

O'Keefe David (1994) 'Union citizenship', in David O'Keefe & Patrick M. Twomey (eds), *Legal Issues of the Maastricht Treaty*, London: Chancery Law Publishing, pp. 87–107

Pescatore Pierre (1974) *The Law of Integration: Emergence of a new Phenomenon in International Relations, based on the Experience of the European Communities*, Leiden: A.W.Sijthoff

Phelan Diarmuid Rossa (1997) *Revolt or Revolution: The Constitutional Boundaries of the European Community*, Dublin: Round Hall Sweet & Maxwell

Pierson Paul (1996/Apr) 'The path to European integration: a historical institutionalist analysis', *Comparative Political Studies*, 29(2), pp. 123–63

Rasmussen Hjalte (1986) *On Law and Policy in the European Court of Justice: A Comparative Study in Judicial Policymaking*, Dordrecht: Martinus Nijhoff

Scheingold Stuart A. (1965) *The Rule of Law in European Integration: The Path of the Schuman Plan*, New Haven: Yale University Press

Scheingold Stuart A. (1971/June) *The Law in Political Integration: the Evolution and Integrative Implications of Regional Legal Processes in the European Community*, Occasional Papers in International Affairs no 27, Center for International Affairs, Harvard University

Scott Joanne (1995) *Development Dilemmas in the European Community: Rethinking Regional Development Policy*, Buckingham: Open University

Sedley Stephen (1991) 'Free speech for Rupert Murdoch', *London Review of Books*, 19 December, pp. 3–5

Shapiro Martin (1992) 'The European Court of Justice', in Alberta M Sbragia (ed.), *Euro-Politics: Institutions and Policymaking in the 'New' European Community*, Washington DC: Brookings Institution, pp. 123–56

Shaw Jo (1994) 'Twin-track Europe – the inside track', in David O'Keefe & Patrick M. Twomey (eds), *Legal Issues of the Maastricht Treaty*, London: Chancery Law Publishing, pp. 295–311

Shaw Jo (1996) *European Community Law*, 2nd ed., Basingstoke: Macmillan

Shaw Jo & More Gillian (eds) (1995) *New Legal Dynamics of European Union*, Oxford: Clarendon Press

Snyder Francis (1990) *New Directions in European Com-Omunity Law*, London: Weidenfeld & Nicolson

Stein Eric (1981) 'Lawyers, judges, and the making of a transnational constitution', *American Journal of International Law*, 75, pp. 1–27

Steiner Josephine & Woods Lorna (1996) *Textbook on EC Law*, London: Blackstone Press

Twomey Patrick M. (1994) 'The European Union: three pillars without a human rights foundation', in David O'Keefe & Patrick M. Twomey (eds), *Legal Issues of the Maastricht Treaty*, London: Chancery Law Publishing, pp. 121–32

Volcansek Mary (1992/July) 'The European Court of Justice: supranational policy-making', *West European Politics*, 15(2), pp. 109–21

Ward Ian (1996a) *A Critical Introduction to European Law*, London: Butterworths

Ward Ian (1996b) *The Margins of European Law*, London: Macmillan

Weatherill Stephen (1995) *Law and Integration in the European Union*, Oxford: Clarendon Press

Weiler J.H.H. (1982a) 'Community, member states and European integration: is the law relevant?', *Journal of Common Market Studies*, 21, pp. 39–56

Weiler J.H.H. (1982b) 'The Community system: the dual character of supranationalism', *Yearbook of European Law*, pp. 267–306

Weiler J.H.H. (1983/Dec) 'Journey to an unknown destination: a retrospective and prospective of the European Court of Justice in the arena of political integration', *Journal of Common Market Studies*, 31(4), pp. 417–46

Weiler J.H.H. (1987) 'The Court of Justice on trial (review of Rasmussen)', *Common Market Law Review*, 24, pp. 555–89

Weiler J.H.H. (1991) 'The transformation of Europe', *Yale Law Journal*, 100, pp. 2403–83

Weiler J.H.H. (1997) 'The Reform of European Constitutionalism', *Journal of Common Market Studies,* 35(1), pp. 97–131

Weiler J.H.H., Haltern Ulrich R. & Mayer Franz C. (1995/July) 'European democracy and its critique', *West European Politics,* 18(3), pp. 4–39

Weiler J.H.H. & Lockhart J.S. (1995) '"Taking rights seriously" seriously: the European Court and its fundamental rights jurisprudence – Parts I and II', *Common Market Law Review,* 32, pp. 51–94; 579–627

Wincott David (1996) 'The Court of Justice and the European policy process', in Jeremy Richardson (ed.), *European Union: Power and Policymaking,* London: Routledge, pp. 170–84

# Other Titles in the Series

Other titles available in the series include:

*Unemployment and Employment Policies in the EU*
*Secrecy, Democracy and the Third Pillar of the European Union*
*The EU and Ethnic Minorities and Migrants at the Workplace*
*The 1996-97 Intergovernmental Conference*
*EU-East Asia Economic Relations: Completing the Triangle?*
*Ukraine and the EU*
*Social Europe: A New Model of Welfare?*
*Alternative Paths to Monetary Union*
*Gender and Citizenship in the EU*

Further information on all titles in the series is available from the publishers at the undermentioned address:

Kogan Page Limited
120 Pentonville Road
London N1 9JN